Travel to Sardinia Island, Italy
History and Information, Holiday, Tourism

Author
Sadic Jordan

Copyright Notice

Copyright © 2017 Global Print Digital
All Rights Reserved

Digital Management Copyright Notice. This Title is not in public domain, it is copyrighted to the original author, and being published by **Global Print Digital**. No other means of reproducing this title is accepted, and none of its content is editable, neither right to commercialize it is accepted, except with the consent of the author or authorized distributor. You must purchase this Title from a vendor who's right is given to sell it, other sources of purchase are not accepted, and accountable for an action against. We are happy that you understood, and being guided by these terms as you proceed. Thank you

First Printing: 2017.

ISBN: 978-1-912483-56-3

Publisher: Global Print Digital.
Arlington Row, Bibury, Cirencester GL7 5ND
Gloucester
United Kingdom.
Website: www.homeworkoffer.com
.

Table of Content

Introduction 1
  Geography 4
Sardinia History for Tourism 11
  The Nuraghic Palace of Barumini 16
  Sardinia: The Nuraghi Island 21
  The Nuragic Village of Serra Orrios Dorgali 25
  The nuraghic Palace of Barumini 28
  Cabu Abbas Riu Mulinu Nuraghe Olbia Sardinia 33
  Nuraghe Losa 36
  Trekking to Tiscali 40
  Su Monte e ape Giants Tomb 43
  S'Ena E Thomes Giants' Tomb - Dorgali 48
  Sa Testa Sacred Well 52
  Santa Cristina Sacred Well 56
  Orune: Su Tempiesu 58
  Ozieri Town 61
  Sassari City 64
  The Nuraghis 66
  Torralba 69
  Arzachena 71
  Bonnanaro 73
  The Sacred Wells 74
  Oristano 77
  Ancient Town of Galtellì. 78
  Olbia - Monti 81
  Mamoiada 87
The People and Culture 90

Ream Mythical People *92*
Religious feasts and rural cults *95*
Art and Archaeology *96*

Travel Information Guide **103**
Discover the island *103*
Tourist Attraction *107*
Protected Marine Areas *110*
The Natural Parks *114*
    North Sardinia 114
    Centre of Sardinia 118
    South Sardinia 121
Beaches in Sardinia *125*
    Costa Smeralda & North East 127
    Alghero & North West 132
    Southern Sardinia 134
Getting Around *138*
Places *142*
    Cagliari 142
    Nuoro 145
    Tortolì 148
    Villasimius 151
    Chia 155
    Castelsardo 157
    Stintino 161
    Bosa 163
    Alghero 165
Weather *168*
Discover the island: Typical Products *171*

Introduction

About Sardinia

Sardinia - Sardegna in Italian - is a large island in the Mediterranean to the west of Italy. It has a mountainous interior and a famed coastline with turquoise waters which attracts throngs of holiday-makers every year. The island is a region of Italy, and its regional capital is Cagliari, on the southern coast. With three international airports and ferries from mainland Italy, it is a very accessible tourist destination.

The island has a long and intriguing history, and is dotted with interesting archaeological sites. In the

Bronze Age the island was populated by an enigmatic people who built *nuraghi* - stone towers - across the island, along with palaces, sacred wells and other structures. Many remain, as ruins, and the importance of these sites is recognised with a UNESCO World Heritage listing.

As Sardinia is on Mediterranean trading routes, various subsequent civilisations colonised or conquered the coastal areas, including the Phoenicians, Romans and Byzantines. Later the island was for some time under Spanish domination. A version of Catalan is still spoken in Alghero. The mountains inland, difficult to conquer and offering little to invaders, have a reputation as untouched pockets of ancient culture and tradition.

Sardinia has a dual reputation within Italy. It is one of the most popular summer holiday destinations for beach-loving Italian families - indeed, it's said that whole districts of Romans decamp with their neighbours to the same Sardinian beaches each August. At the same time , Sardinia's ancient 'otherness' casts a lingering and occasionally sinister shadow: the shepherds and hardy inland communities, the mountains once seen as the lair of kidnappers and the enduring individual character and dialects of Sardinia all make the place rather un-Italian. None of this, however, affects the tourists who flock to the white beaches and blue seas.

The smartest destination in Sardinia is the Costa Smeralda, the 'emerald coast'. This beautiful stretch of coastline at Sardinia's north-east corner was developed in the 1960s by wealthy investors including the Aga Khan. Every summer gossip magazines are full of photos of Italian and international 'celebrities' partying, swimming or hanging out on huge yachts in Porto Cervo and the other exclusive resorts of the Costa Smeralda.

Sardinia isn't all glitz, though. The island has many beaches and stretches of coast which are largely unspoiled and plenty of down-to-earth towns and resorts. Lagoon, island and mountain habitats all feature among the region's nature reserves, where you can see a wide range of wildlife including flamingoes, golden eagles, mountain goats and wild white donkeys.

Geography
Ancient and amazing land
Sardinia lies in central Mediterranean Sea, between Corsica and the Tunisian coasts. Its provinces are Cagliari (chief city), Olbia-Tempio, Sassari, Nuoro, Tortolì-Lanusei (Ogliastra), Carbonia-Iglesias, Sanluri-Villacidro (Medio Campidano) and Oristano. After Sicily, it is the biggest Mediterranean island with its 24,090 sq/km, including all its minor islands. The furthest distances are 270 km North (Capo Falcone) and South (Capo Teulada); 145 km East (Capo Comino)

South-West (Capo dell'Argentiera). Sardinia is amazingly nearer to North Africa than Italy!

The Eastern part is mainly mountainous, with granite stones especially in Gallura; the Western is more heterogeneous, with basalt and trachyte plains, many mineral deposits in the South (Sulcis Iglesiente). Campidano, the island's biggest plain, lies between the Cagliari and Oristano gulfs. There are no mountain chains except for Gennargentu with the island's highest peak, Punta la Marmora, (1834 m).

The Sardinian coast of 1,897 km (equal to a quarter of Italy) consists of high and steep reefs, especially in the North-East (Capo Caccia and Bosa) and in the South, with inlets that host some of the sandiest beaches of the Mediterranean.

Sardinia hasn't got any natural lakes, with only one exception constituted by the Baratz small lake situated in the oriental Nurra plain, under the "dell'Acqua"

Mountain, and it has a maximum depth of only 20 meters. Neverthless, the artificial lakes are quite numerous, and carried out to collect the countless streams, which have a torrential character, often swell and impetuous in winter and quite dry in the summer.

The lakes which are more representative for their extension are:

- Omodeo lake, due to the barrage of Tirso river. In 1923, when the barrage was constructed, it represented the biggest dam in the world which gathered the widest artificial lake in Europe.

- Coghinas lake, arises from the obstruction of Coghinas river. This dam has been built in 1927 to satisfy hydroelectric functions.

- Flumendosa lake is placed in the territory of Villanova Strisaili, in the Southern slopes of Gennargentu. This lake originates from the Flumendosa river; it satisfies hydroelectric and irrigation functions.

- Gusana lake: it derives from the barrage of Gusana torrent, nearby Gavoi, where a 320 metres long dam was built.

- Flumendosa-Arcu S.Stefano lake: it is due to the damming of the Flumendosa nearby Orroli.

- Mulargia lake: it originates from the stopping of Mulargia torrent before its confluence with Flumendosa river.

The other lakes: Liscia Lake, Cedrino Lake.

The hydrographical network is formed by four main rivers, the Tirso, the Flumendosa, the Coghinas and the Flumini Mannu which run towards the four littorals sea for a total length of 9.963 km.

The Tirso, whose ancient name was Thyrsus, is the major Sardinian river. It is 159 km long, while the basin size is 3.375 kmq., and flows into the Oristano gulf. It rises in the granite upland of Buddusò at a height of 900 meters. Still in the Western coast, but in the North side of Tirso basin the stream Temo flows and at a distance of four kilometres from its mouth, where Bosa village is, its bed grows larger and larger till it becomes navigable. That's why it's been created a small river port in Bosa Marina. The Flumendosa, which has its source in the huge massif of Gennargentu, is the Sardinian most important river, not just for its length (122 km), or for the width of the basin (1.826 kmq) but for the invaluable contribute that its water gives to the island economy.

or for the width of the basin (1.826 kmq) but for the invaluable contribute that its water gives to the island economy. From Gennargentu it rises also the Cedrino, not very long (70 km) but among the most reach in water. The Coghinas, whose ancient name is Thermus, is formed at the confluence of two rivers coming from two different directions, Rio Mannu (Berchidda) and Rio Mannu (Ozieri). Flumini Mannu is the fourth river, with a length of about 86 km and runs till the Western coast near Oristano

The flag

A red-cross and four blindfolded moors, this is the symbol of the Sardinian people.

Its origin is vague, stemming perhaps from King Peter of Aragon celebrating the victory of Alcoraz (1096) and symbolizing the help in battle of San Giorgio (red cross on white background) and the moor's (Arab kings) heads cut off in battle.

In the mid XIV century the four moors were firstly linked to Sardinia, thus representing the kingdom within the Confederation of Aragon's Crown (Gerle Coat of Arms).

The moors' heads were represented in different ways: turning left, right, uncovered, crowned, blindfolded.

Presently, the four moors, wary of Piedmontese' "illiberal" behavior toward the Sardinian People, have turned their heads and opened their eyes, no longer blindfolded.

The flag is also the symbol of the Partito Sardo d'Azione, the former Nationalist Party founded after the First World War with the intention of defending the Sardinian identity and protecting the island's cultural aspects such as promotion and teaching of the Sardinian language.

Sardinia History for Tourism

The first settlements in Sardinia:

The human presence in Sardinia dates back to the early Palaeolithic Age (between 500.000 and 100.000 years ago). The first civilization come to life during the Neolithic Age (6000 - 2700 B.C.), it was called Bonu-Ighinu (till 3500 B.C.), then Ozieri or San Michele (till 2700 B.C). During the Neolithic age Sardinians used to live in caves and, besides hunting, they were engaged in agriculture, fishing and breeding. They excelled in the art of pottery, weaving and sculpture. The first Megalithic and funeral architectural monuments (dolmen, menhir and domus de janas) date back to this

Age. During the late Neolithic Age (till 1600 B.C.) the Monte Claro and the Bonnanaro civilization came to life. These people used to forge copper and, subsequently, bronze tools.

The Nuragic civilization:

The Nuragic civilization developed between the Bronze Age and the Iron Age (from 1800 to 500 B.C.). Almost 8000 nuraghes, about 400 tombs of Giantsand no specified number of sacred wells are examples of the impressiveness of the nuragic civilization. The so-called bronzetti (representing little modern ships) and the archaeological finds (such as the representations of Shardana people in the Egyptian temple of Medinet Abu) demonstrate how the nuraghic people dominated the whole Mediterranean area. The theories of Sergio Frau, a journalist and writer of the book "Le Colonne d'Ercole, un'inchiesta" (The Pillars of Hercules. An investigation) state that Sardinia actually was the powerful Island of Atlantis. Eminent scholars and archaeologists of all over the world maintain these theories.

The Phoenician Age:
Between the X and the VIII centuries B.C the Phoenician civilization chose Sardinia as the crucial point for its commerce. After a long period of good relationship, about 535 B.C. the most powerful Carthaginians tried to conquer the Island. At the end of the same century, after fierce fights, they conquered the Island. Under the Carthage domination some new important settlements such as Karalis (the current Cagliari), Nora, Solki (sant'Antioco), Bosa and Tharros came to life.

The Roman Age:
After a long struggle between Romans and the Sardinian-Phoenician people, Rome managed to conquer Sardinia to dominate it definitely in 214 B.C The cohabitation with Sardinians wasn't easy mainly

because Romans were considered the conqueror enemies. Anyway, after long struggles, Sardinia became the barn of Rome.

The Byzantium Age:

After the collapse of the Roman Empire, Sardinia was invaded from Vandals who remained in the Island about 80 years, till the seizure of Byzantium in 534 B.C.. The Byzantine domination deeply influenced Sardinian civilization to such an extent that they inculcated the cult of Emperor Constantine (Santu Antine). Every year in Sedilo, people compete in a horse riding called s'Ardia in honour of him.

From the Vandals to the marine repubblic:

In the IX century, the Sardinians, after having driven the Vandals away for several times, won their independence and organized themselves politically, by establishing local governments called "Giudicati" (Ancient Kingdoms of Sardinia). This kind of organization lasted for a long time and there is still evidence of this in Sardinian law, originally introduced by Judge Eleonora D'Arborea's "Carta de logu": namely a set of norms.

In the XI century, Sardinia needed help from Geneva and Pisa Maritime Republics to defend itself from the Arabs who were finally defeated in 1016. The Republic of Pisa thus gained sovereignty over the island especially from an artistic and commercial viewpoint, rather than in politics which remained in the hands of the Giudicati.

From the Aragoneses to sardinian reign:

During the XIV century, the Aragonese started ruling in Sardinia and, soon, following the merger between the families of Castilla and Aragon, this translated into the Spanish occupation, replacing local governments with a feudal system under Spanish noble families.

As Spain declined, Sardinia passed in the hands of the Hapsburg family (1714) and, after four years, to the Savoy dukedom. The Piedmontese occupied it in 1720. Under their rule, feudalism was abolished (1835). In 1847 island autonomy was abolished and Sardinia-Piedmontese, the first core area of the Italy Kingdom, was formed accordingly.

First world war to nowadays:
After the end of the war, the Partito Sardo d'Azione, which would represent the people's needs and autonomy, was formed. With the advent of Fascism, further intervention included the construction of basins and the Tirso Dam, nevertheless, the economy remained weak.

Only the granting of the Special Autonomy and Statute of the Region (1947) boosted the island's economy.

The Nuraghic Palace of Barumini

The tower people invaded Sardinia. They did that with the Nuraghi, scattered on the whole territory. There's no corner of the coast and inland without evidence of the presence of the nuraghic people. A mysterious civilization that left in Barumini one of the most magnificent example of the architecture of the past.

Until the first half of the twentieth century, between the villages of Barumini and Tuili (at the foot of the Giara of Gesturi), there was a peculiar hill. People were not amazed by its shape, but by the presence of a small window. Many myths and tales went around, sometimes they were created to make sure children didn't go near that mysterious place.

A young archaeologist from Barumini, named Giovanni Lilliu, asked for permission to excavate, to find out what was hidden underneath the hill and most of all beneath that little window.

Works started in 1951 and Lilliu himself didn't expect to discover such an incredible treasure.

Hidden 30 metres underground was Su Nuraxi(the nuraghe) a stone giant, amazing evidence of the nuraghic civilization.

The Palace of Barumini overlooks the surrounding flat land and is formed by a huge quatrefoiled nuraghe, whose central tower is its oldest construction. Originally it was almost 20 metres high and divided into three floors. The tower should date back to 1478 B.C.(the Bronze Age) and was probably quite imposing. The four towers surrounding the central one should date back to the 13th century B.C. Between the two constructions there was an inner courtyard that linked the central tower to the other four (each tower is positioned according to the cardinal points). Within the courtyard there's a 20 metres deep well that still holds drinking-water, confirming how the nuraghic civilization had remarkable architectural knowledge.

Around the 11th century B.C the entire complex (the central keep and the quatrefoiled bastion) was surrounded by a 3 metres thick circle of walls to reinforce and better defend the palace.

From that moment on entering the fortress became even more difficult for all invaders: the only possible entrance was a small opening placed at a height of 7 metres. During the following years other seven towers were built around the palace making the construction even more imposing.

Around the palace there are many nuraghic huts, with very narrow alleys and an evolved urbanistic structure. The excavations showed how the village kept expanding for centuries. During the Iron Age (8th century B.C.) "the council hut" (a construction with a circular seat and some recesses in the walls) must have been the centre of the village activity.

The nuraghic Palace of Barumini was such a grand fortress, that every population that dominated this territory chose it as their bulwark.

But it was thanks to the 30 metres of ground that buried it that its fate has become so mysterious.

According to journalist Sergio Frau, who wrote the book "le Colonne d'Ercole. Un'inchiesta" (Hercules' Columns. An investigation), Su Nuraxi could have been swept away by a giant wave, that, from the Gulf of Cagliari, covered the whole Campidano (the region south of Barumini) and swallowed the palace. A catastrophic event that would explain why many nuraghi of the area are partially destroyed only on the side facing the Gulf of Cagliari.

Sergio Frau's fascinating theory goes as far as identifying Sardinia as the ancient island of Atlas (which became famous with the name of Atlantis) and started a big debate in the academic world. Lilliu himself (who called Su Nuraxi "the downcast giant") confessed that the thesis of the journalist from La Repubblica has firm foundations. Sergio Frau's work led to the creation of an itinerant exhibition (Atlantikà), that was held also in the UNESCO headquarters (Paris) and the Academy of Lincei (Rome).

It was the UNESCO (United Nations Educational, Scientific and Cultural Organization) that in 1997 recognized Su Nuraxi as a World Heritage.

Sardinia: The Nuraghi Island

If the afterlife exists, probably an entire population observes Sardinia and smiles.

This population is the nuragic population which observes people who try to interpret the Tombs of the Giants, the Nuragic Wells, the holy sources and the Nuraghi.

The Nuragic civilization developed between the Bronze Age and the Iron Age (from 1800 to 500 B.C.). 8000 nuraghes, about 400 tombs of Giants and no specified number of sacred wells are examples of the impressiveness of the nuragic civilization. The so-called bronzetti (representing little modern ships) and the archaeological finds (such as the representations of Shardana people in the Egyptian temple of Medinet Abu) demonstrate how the nuraghic people dominated the whole Mediterranean area. The theories of Sergio Frau, a journalist and writer of the book "Le Colonne d'Ercole, un'inchiesta" (The Pillars of Hercules. An investigation) state that Sardinia actually was the powerful Island of Atlas (also called Atlantis). Eminent scholars and archaeologists of all over the world maintain these theories.

THE NURAGHES => Historical period: bronze age - iron age (1800/1000 BC)

Sardinia counts at least 8000 ancient towers made with stones; in the past it was possible to count 20000 constructions like these. We wonder why this advanced, civil and powerful population used to spend time building towers. We wonder if their aim was religious, military or if they used to build these constructions in order to live there. Maybe we will not be able to give an answer to these questions and this is why it seems that the nuragic people laugh from the afterlife.

THE TOMBS OF GIANTS => Historical period: around the Early Bronze Age (2000 B.C.)

The Tombs of Giants, so called because of their gigantic dimensions, are another typical element of Sardinia's megalithic period. Usually the frontal part of their structure is delimited by some sort of semicircle (exedra), almost as to symbolize a bull's horns. Viewed from above the shape of the Tombs of Giants brings to mind that of an uterus or a woman in labour. This interpretation would confirm how closely connected life and death were for nuraghic people and how their megalithism was linked to the cult of fecundation.

THE SACRED WELLS > Historical period: end of bronze age-beginning of iron age (1500/900 BC)

The nuragic wells are similar to the nuraghi's architectural structure but they have been built underground. The wells had many symbols. They represented the female sexual organs like if they were the entrance and the exit towards the afterworld.

The Nuragic Village of Serra Orrios Dorgali

Location: Middle- east Sardinia, 10km from Dorgali, in the Province of Nuoro.

Period: Nuraghic Age From Medium Bronze Age to Iron Age (15th 9th centuries B.C.).

If someone had supposed that the nuraghi were just houses, here is the proof of their mistake: Serra Orrios. (in the middle of Gollei basaltic tableland, 10km from Dorgali) one of Sardinia's biggest nuragic villages.

Could the nuraghe have been the palace of the Shepherd King? Looking at Serra Orrios conglomeration, even this hypothesis seems to be without foundation. The closest nuraghe to the village is indeed located at about 500 metres. Which king, however haughty and arrogant , would be so unwary to isolate himself from the rest of the population? An enemy attack would have found him quite defenceless. Could then the nuraghe have been the house of the priest? The nuragic village of Serra Orrios consists of a hundred huts and two megaron temples (with an elongated rectangular shape and a vestibule preceding the cell).

The possibility that the priest was a character that would arrive to one of the temples and then go back to his nuragic fortress can not be ruled out. A fascinating hypothesis, but why in the case of Barumini is the nuraghe surrounded by huts? Was the priest of Serra Orrio less humble than the one of Su Nuraxi? Once again the nuragic civilization forces us to draw endless comparisons and ask thousands of questions with as many replies. All hypothetically right, none objectively correct.

Then let's try to understand these people better, hoping to find inspiration from their world, their houses, their streets. The village of Serra Orrios is the perfect place to observe the degree of organization of nuragic people. The built-up area, that could probably have about 300 inhabitants, has a very complex structure, almost "protourban", with narrow streets, small squares and wells. Every construction has been made with basaltic rocks with "dry walling" technique.

Many finds have been discovered in the village (they are exposed at the Archaeological Museum of Dorgali) and they document how the inhabitants engaged primarily in stock farming and agriculture. The loom weights, whorls and reels show instead the practice of spinning and weaving, while moulds and foundryman's pliers document metal processing.

The village can be accessed from the south, passing an elliptical shaped wall hedge that delimits an area with a small megaron temple. Probably this temple used to accommodate foreigners. Located far from the huts, the sacred construction had a rectangular plan and the entrance is oriented towards east-south-east.

Close to the huts there is another irregular rectangular hedge that contains another small megaron temple, the bigger one. The temple can be accessed through a south-east located architrave-opening, reachable only after passing a second entrance.

The built-up area, about 3 metres from the second temple, is composed of circular huts. Among these huts one stand out from the village, the so-called "hut of meetings", whose entrance is located at north-east.

The nuraghic Palace of Barumini

The tower people invaded Sardinia. They did that with the Nuraghi, scattered on the whole territory. There's no corner of the coast and inland without evidence of the presence of the nuraghic people. A mysterious civilization that left in Barumini one of the most magnificent example of the architecture of the past.

Until the first half of the twentieth century, between the villages of Barumini and Tuili (at the foot of the Giara of Gesturi), there was a peculiar hill. People were not amazed by its shape, but by the presence of a small window. Many myths and tales went around, sometimes they were created to make sure children didn't go near that mysterious place.

A young archaeologist from Barumini, named Giovanni Lilliu, asked for permission to excavate, to find out what was hidden underneath the hill and most of all beneath that little window. Works started in 1951 and Lilliu himself didn't expect to discover such an incredible treasure.

Hidden 30 metres underground was Su Nuraxi(the nuraghe) a stone giant, amazing evidence of the nuraghic civilization. The Palace of Barumini overlooks the surrounding flat land and is formed by a huge quatrefoiled nuraghe, whose central tower is its oldest construction. Originally it was almost 20 metres high and divided into three floors. The tower should date back to 1478 B.C.(the Bronze Age) and was probably quite imposing. The four towers surrounding the central one should date back to the 13th century B.C. Between the two constructions there was an inner courtyard that linked the central tower to the other four (each tower is positioned according to the cardinal points). Within the courtyard there's a 20 metres deep well that still holds drinking-water, confirming how the nuraghic civilization had remarkable architectural knowledge.

Around the 11th century B.C the entire complex (the central keep and the quatrefoiled bastion) was surrounded by a 3 metres thick circle of walls to reinforce and better defend the palace.

From that moment on entering the fortress became even more difficult for all invaders: the only possible entrance was a small opening placed at a height of 7 metres. During the following years other seven towers were built around the palace making the construction even more imposing.

Around the palace there are many nuraghic huts, with very narrow alleys and an evolved urbanistic structure. The excavations showed how the village kept expanding for centuries. During the Iron Age (8th century B.C.) "the council hut" (a construction with a circular seat and some recesses in the walls) must have been the centre of the village activity.

The nuraghic Palace of Barumini was such a grand fortress, that every population that dominated this territory chose it as their bulwark.

But it was thanks to the 30 metres of ground that buried it that its fate has become so mysterious.

According to journalist Sergio Frau, who wrote the book "le Colonne d'Ercole. Un'inchiesta" (Hercules' Columns. An investigation), Su Nuraxi could have been swept away by a giant wave, that, from the Gulf of Cagliari, covered the whole Campidano (the region south of Barumini) and swallowed the palace. A catastrophic event that would explain why many nuraghi of the area are partially destroyed only on the side facing the Gulf of Cagliari.

Sergio Frau's fascinating theory goes as far as identifying Sardinia as the ancient island of Atlas (which became famous with the name of Atlantis) and started a big debate in the academic world. Lilliu himself (who called Su Nuraxi "the downcast giant") confessed that the thesis of the journalist from La Repubblica has firm foundations. Sergio Frau's work led to the creation of an itinerant exhibition (Atlantikà), that was held also in the UNESCO headquarters (Paris) and the Academy of Lincei (Rome).

It was the UNESCO (United Nations Educational, Scientific and Cultural Organization) that in 1997 recognized Su Nuraxi as a World Heritage.

Cabu Abbas Riu Mulinu Nuraghe Olbia Sardinia

Historical period: 1600 - 1300 BC

The nuragic culture is one of the most attractive and mysterious as the nuragic people left in a little territory like Sardinia lots of mysteries. The world has today many archaeological doubts, if we think about the Egyptian pyramids or the Mayan pyramids, the Easter Island's statues, the Nazca lines in Perù...Many and wonderful mysteries which excite all along the most curious people.

But Sardinia has many archaeological mysteries: Tombs of Giants, Menhirs, Domus de Janas, Dolmens, Sacred Wells, Holy Sources and Nuraghi. We can find these megalithic constructions everywhere in the island. In the past it was possible to count more than 20000 constructions, now there are only 8000 sites. The number is approximate, there are probably ancient towers underground, as in the Barumini archaeological site, completely hidden 30 metres underground and discovered in 1955.

The nuragic constructions (nuraghi) are towers built with false domes (tholos) according to a particular technique. Nuraghi are built by laying big stones of similar size on top of each other leaving a cavity in the middle. It can be assumed that the nuragic people used to build on steep banks starting with big stones and then reducing their dimensions. The biggest towers could reach 20 metres and at the top of them it was probably present a terrace (protected by a parapet) reachable thanks to a helicoidal staircase. In order to have the light they used to leave some slits among the stones. The entrance was faced south and it was followed by a corridor to the main room.

One of the most interesting nuraghi in the north of Sardinia is the nuraghe of Cabu Abbas (named also Riu Mulinu) which is located near Olbia. It is particular especially for its position. As a matter of fact it s located on a rocky promontory which dominates the gulf of Olbia at a sea level of 246 metres. When you reach the nuraghe you can imagine the reason why nuragic people chose this place: it is possible to have a great view so we can assume that they used this construction in order to check the arrival of enemy boats. But probably the nuraghe was used for other aims like religious aims (we can think about the cult of water). This explains the finding, during the excavations of 1936, of a nuragic bronze which represents a woman with an amphora on her head.

The nuragic complex of Cabu Abbas is characterized by the presence of a big wall 220 metres long and 5 metres high and wide. Its structure incorporates the rocky spikes present in the area. The wall had two entrances: one on the North side and one on the South side.

Inside there is the little circular nuraghe with only one tower. It has been realized with granite stones and it is characterized by a passage which has on its right a little niche and on its left the stair to the upper floor which has been destroyed. The central room has two parallel niches and a well 3 metres deep.

Nuraghe Losa

PERIOD: Nuragic Age Middle Bronze Age (Fifteen and Fourteen centuries B.C.).

The nuraghe "Losa" is one of the stone giants that led archaeologists and scholars to think that nuraghi were used to protect nuragic people from enemy attacks.

Its structure is surely impressive, since its highest tower is still 13 metres high. Originally the nuragic complex was even more imposing, and that is one of the reasons why the military hypothesis has convinced the most important scholars for years. But is it really possible? Could the nuraghi have been defensive bulwarks?

Obviously military techniques have changed during the centuries, but some things stay the same. So it is not clear, why, during an enemy attack, nuragic people chose to find shelter inside the nuraghi. The nuraghe "Losa", although gigantic, does not seem like the ideal place to be used as a refuge by dozens and dozens of people. Even because any invading people could easily win simply waiting.

Why is the structure of Nuraghe "Losa" similar to a fortress? Why did people build a giant construction with huge basalt blocks? And why was it built in different stages, if not to strengthen its defences?

The nuraghe was initially made of just one main tower. Only later three more towers were built, linked by an external wall that surrounds the whole construction. Nuraghe "Losa" is also one of the few ones without an inner courtyard and this represents another element to doubt about the possibility that the building had a defensive purpose. Even because the courtyard usually had a water well. How can you take refuge in a fortress without water supply?

Let's try to analyse other hypothesis, like the one that sees nuraghi as connected to religious symbolisms. As in the major part of nuraghi and even in the "Losa", the main entrance is located on the South-East side. Inside, through a straight corridor, you enter the central tower, whose upper floor can still be visited through a staircase cut into the wall. The same corridor leads to the two side towers.

The rear tower can be reached from a secondary entrance, in this case north-east located. Was then Nuraghe "Losa" a huge religious monument? Were nuraghi worship places dedicated to the Mother Goddess? Some scholars maintain that their structure resembles that of a maternal womb. The entrance would be located on the South-East side in order to be more connected to the sunlight, considered the male fertilizing strength. This interpretation would explain the orientation of a large part of nuraghi, with an often south/south-east located entrance. But it would not clear up some doubts. Why would the "Losa" have so many "wombs", all of different sizes? Twin birth? And why is the entrance of one of these "wombs" independent and located on the north-east side?

It is clear that the nuraghi enigma is far from a solution. And this is their greatest attraction.

The interpretations that consider them huge funeral monuments clash with others that are more pragmatic and pseudo-scientific and see them as large furnaces to melt metals, or primitive warehouses to store food.

There is no way out: those who visit nuraghi always have a theory and, as it happens when admiring an artistic masterpiece, everyone is convinced they have found the solution to the enigma around them. It is the great thing about the nuraghi; it is the great thing about Nuraghe "Losa"

Trekking to Tiscali

Ideal for: families with children, young people, people who love trekking

Behind Mount Corrasi, in the Oliena's area (NU) is one of the most mysterious example of ancient human settlement. Visiting Tiscali is an adventure that will make you go back to the nuraghic civilization.

It's a journey that doesn't give you answers, on the contrary, it increases the enigmas about the civilizations that occupied Sardinia and left thousand of unaccountable and fantastic signs. Furthermore, Tiscali archaeological findings are different from all the other mysterious ones left by the nuraghi people. The Nuraghes used to be clearly visible, rarely hidden; Tiscali, on the contrary, is a secret fort which can be seen only when in front of its entrance.

Tiscali, a 518 metres high mountain, rises at the bottom of the enchanting and wild Lanaitto valley. Hidden at the top of the mountain is a huge round open-air cave. Once inside you will enjoy the wonderful view of a beautiful masonry huts village. The nuraghes agglomeration was so wide that it was divided into two different districts.

This village was discovered by people who came after the nuraghic civilization and from that moment on it was considered an ideal place where to live. People lived here until the Roman and the High Middle Age, even though it was "rediscovered" by accident only at the end of the 20th century. Despite the continuous pillages, Tiscali remains one of the most fascinating and charming ancient settlement of all the Mediterranean area.

FLORA:

asphodel, phoenician juniper, evergreen oak, rock rose, lentisk, arbutus, turpentine tree and phyllirea.

FAUNA:

mammals: mouflon, marten, doormouse, wild cat, Sardinian wild-boar, Sardinian deer, fallow-deer, wild rabbit, weasel, hare, savi's pygmy shrew, hedgehog, Sardinian white-toothed shrew, European free-tailed bat, bet-winged bat, greater horseshoe bat, brown long-eared bat, Sardinian brown long-eared bat, kuhl's pipistrelle bat, savi's pipistrelle bat, pipistrelle and other species of bat.

amphibian: tyrrhenian painted frog, sardinian mountain newt, Sardinian tree-frog.

Birds: golden eagle, bonelli eagle, vulture (griffon vulture), barn owl, woodcock, lark, little owl, chough and many other species of little birds.

Reptiles: coluber, grass snake, Sardinian ocellated skink, Italian wall lizard, bedriaga's wall lizard, Tyrrhenian lizard, three-toed skink, grass snake, Hermann's tortoise.

Su Monte e ape Giants Tomb

HISTORICAL PERIOD: From 1800 to 1100 B.C.

Nuraghic people struck again, giving us more doubts and mysteries. We're talking about the Tombs of

Giants: dark megalithic constructions, unique in shape and size, that are scattered throughout the island. So far about 320 have been found, but Sardinia is a continent that uncover itself slowly and we can be sure that its territory is jealously hiding many more Tombs of Giants.

The name of these mysterious monuments comes from ancient popular beliefs and to explain them you have to identify yourself with the populations that, before the flourishing of the archaeological sciences, found themselves in front of these mysterious sights. Try to put yourself in the shoes of those people who were the first to discover these constructions. Imagine being the inhabitants of a land that constantly gives you incredible works from the past.

Try to see huge stone slabs stuck in the ground that form weirdly shaped constructions. Won over by the mystery, you'll start to dig at the least. And how surprised would you be if you found hundreds of human bones? And if you found out that they are stripped of flesh, scratched, scraped and consumed, and then looked again at that huge door that dominates the entire megalithic structure, wouldn't it be easy to think that that construction could have been home to enormous ogres, that used to feast on human flesh and then buried the remains? This is how a myth was born: the myth of Giants.

Not far from "Olbia -Costa Smeralda" Airport is the Tomb of Giants "Su Monte de s'ape". But first let's see what the original structure of one of these nuraghic grave might have looked like. The whole funeral monument was probably covered by a mound of earth and stones. Frontally the construction was delimited by a semicircle (exedra). This was probably the only part that was exposed. In the middle of the exedra was a huge engraved granite stele (4 metres high), with a small opening in its base, probably used as an entrance to the tomb. Inside, the sepulchre was formed by a funerary chamber that usually was between 5 to 15 metres long and no more than 2 metres high.

As for the sacred wells, what surprises most is the shape of these strange constructions. Viewed from above the construction brings to mind the head of a bull, or the stylization of an uterus, but also that of a pelvis and the limbs of a woman in labour. This is the most fascinating interpretation, because the semicircle shape could really represents human legs with an opening to the netherworld in the middle of it. So life and death for nuraghic people were symbolized in the same way, as a motherly entrance to a world and an exit to another. Birth and death that make us all protagonist of the same fate. Maybe that's one of the reasons why the Tombs of Giants housed collective graves, probably without any class distinction. It's possible that they were used as charnel houses that could contain up to 200 skeletons. The Tombs of Giants were also the ideal places for ancient and mysterious religious ceremonies.

The Tomb of Giants "Su Monte e s'ape" keeps these characteristics. Only a part of the central stele remained and is not on site at the moment. The entire structure is 28 metres long and 6 metres wide, while the sepulchral gallery is more than 10 metres long. Thanks to these measurements, "Su Monte e s'ape" can be considered one of the biggest Tombs of Giants in the island. The construction of this funerary monument, as in many other cases, has gone through different phases. The rectangular shape probably dates back to the pre-nuraghic period (Early Bronze Age: 1800-1600 B.C.), with the use of less carved stones and with the only presence of the funerary chamber. Some of the covering slabs might date back to that period as well. In full nuraghic age (around 1600 B.C.) the construction was modified and embellished with new architectural elements. The exedra-shaped monumental front and the covering of the funerary chamber with an external face probably date back to this period.

S'Ena E Thomes Giants' Tomb - Dorgali

Location: Middle-East Sardinia, on the road to Dorgali.
Period: Nuraghic Age Early and Middle Bronze Age (1800 1600 B.C.).

One of the most fascinating mysteries of the nuraghi island is certainly that of the Tombs of Giants. The Tomb of Giants of S'Ena e Thomes is one of the most impressive and intriguing examples, maybe because it is one of the best preserved tombs. S'Ena e Thomes is mighty and imposing, still very similar to what it might have been like thousands of years ago. Its exedra (the semicircle that probably draws a bull's horns) has a width exceeding 10 metres and its central stele is almost 4 metres high and weighs about 7 tons.

These huge dimensions explain why these nuragic funeral monuments have been called "Tombs of Giants". S'Ena e Thomes' funeral corridor is almost intact, with flat-arch covering, that is made of stone slabs laid horizontally along the walls of the corridor.

But who had the honour of being buried in this tomb? If it is true that these monuments used to host collective sepulchres, then the possibility that they were considered real cemeteries is to be excluded. Probably the honour of being buried inside the tomb of giants was not reserved to all the dead people , but it is even true that, judging by the findings, it was noted how the bones were not buried following a hierarchical order. We can so assume that, for nuragic people, death did not discriminate, and who was worthy to be buried inside a tomb of giants, was not worthier than others. So even S'Ena e Thomes confirms how the kingdom of the deads has no regard for anybody.

However, the astronomical orientation of the tomb amazes us once more. The exedra of the major part of the Tombs of Giants is oriented towards south-east, the sunrise direction during the winter solstice. Other tombs look towards east, probably because of the sunrise during the equinoxes. The Tomb of Giants of S'Ena e Thomes however is oriented towards south, maybe in relation to the summer solstice sunset. And then: a research of three scholars of the Astronomical Observatory of Brera's National Institute of Astrophysics (L. Marchisio, A. Manara e A. Gaspani), revealed a big secret. The structure of S'Ena e Thomes, made entirely of granite, has an astronomical azimuth of its axis' orientation which is identical to those of the

Tomb of Giants "Goronna" (in Paulilatino, in the Province of Oristano) and that of Baddu Pirastru (in Thiesi, in the Province of Sassari).

The three Tombs of Giants seem to be oriented towards the star Aldebaran (Alpha Tauri) in the constellation Taurus. As every hypothesis, there is always someone who is sceptical. There will always be someone who say that these megalithic monuments are simple graves as ours. But when the coincidences are so many....well, as they say..."One coincidence is just a coincidence. Two coincidences are a clue. Three coincidences are a proof" Agatha Christie

How to Get There: From Olbia take the SS 131 d.c.n. towards Nuoro, then take the junction to Dorgali. After 4,1 km, a road sign indicates the entrance to the archaeological area .
Park the car and walk for about 400m along the path.

Sa Testa Sacred Well

HISTORICAL PERIOD: 1400-1200 BC

The most beautiful thing that we can experience in our lives is mystery, which is the source of every art and science. The being who does not know this emotion and who is incapable to feel the amazement is dead (Albert Einstein).

When we talk about Sardinia, the isle of the mysteries, we are obliged to mention this sentence, because of the fascinating past of the nuraghi's island. An obscure past, obscure like the darkness of its sacred wells which are softly lightened by a gleam of light. The same gleam which captures the imagination of all the visitors who discover a sacred well. The same gleam which let you say: "I got it", "I know the reason why they were so useful..."but then the intuition disappears and you understand that there are so many doubts...

The nuragic civilization spread on the island many doubts; maybe they wanted to tease people who forgot them. Incredible people who decided not to be forgotten, leaving on the stones these indecipherable signs.

Near the Olbia airport you can find one of this fascinating places: the sacred well of Sa Testa. It is an example of high imagination linked to inexplicable signs. In many parts of the Mediterranean area it is possible to find constructions similar to the sacred wells, but it is difficult to find many constructions like these, or constructions with the same characteristics. During the years, archaeologists and experts have tried with no success to understand why the wells had been built in that particular way and which was the utility.

They have made different suppositions but there are not many certainties. These wells remind us the nuraghi, the difference is that they were built underground. It seems that these constructions wanted to represent the female sexual organs, to underline the entrance and the exit towards the afterworld. According to this interpretation it is possible to imagine that the nuragic people built the holy wells according to the lunar stages.

The holy well of Sa Testa is divided into 4 parts: a circular courtyard, an entrance hall, a staircase and a tholos room (false dome). In this room there is the source with a little crack.

Nuragic people did not make anything by chance. We can talk about one of the mysteries of the well of Sa Testa: number 17. In the structure there are 17 steps and the entire well is 17.17 metres long. The number of the nuragic steps is often different. There are temples with 12, 13 or 25 steps. At the moment it is possible to count in Sardinia 30 holy wells more or less. The number 17 is a very important number for the nuragic culture. The ancient Sardinian population, which is supposed to correspond to the glorious civilization of the Shardana, used to make for the young, feasts that could be considered initiation rituals. They used to celebrate the young aged 3,7,13 and 17 years.

3 years: it was possible to see and understand the differences between males and females' behaviour and character.

7 years: they were celebrated because at this age the child started to become independent and to make his first experiences.

13 years: the males started to become men and the females could become mothers.

17 years: it was the most important stage. The young started to become completely independent. It was the beginning of an independent social life, a life of freedom and responsibilities.

Maybe the 17 steps indicated the introduction to society but this is just one of the suppositions...this does not matter. We can still be attracted by the mistery.

Santa Cristina Sacred Well

LOCATION: Santa Cristina archaeological site is located on a basaltic plateau near Abbasanta, in the west-central Sardinia.

PERIOD: Nuragic period - Late Bronze Age (between IX and XI century B.C)

Santa Cristina area, near Paulilatino (OR), is one of the most beatiful Sardinian archaeological sites. The major complex includes a nuragic holy well, a nurage and nuragic habitations. Santa Cristina nuragic well, due to its mysterious appeal and inexplicable coincidences, is probably the most known holy well.

Sacred Wells had initially a circular compound wall, like Su Tempiesu holy well. Why does the moon light reflect in the well every 18 years and 6 months between December and the beginning of January? Is it only an incredible coincidence? Or did the well wall have a perpendicular opening on the top? Enigmas of the nuragic culture; fascinating mysteries with no solution.

Another enigma: In the past, during vernal and autumnal equinoxes, the sun shone down the steps through the hole in the stone construction over the well. It happened when the earth's axis was tilted and Rigel Kent(even called Alfa Centauri, the closest star of the system) was visible from the island. The sun and the moon, one more together, relate to the nuragic sites.

Santa Cristina refers to the little rural church near the well, surrounded by small habitations (called

Muristenes o Cumbessias), used by faithful people to celebrate the saint on the second Sunday in May and the Archangel Gabriel on the forth Sunday in October .

The basalt holy well constists (as the other sardinian and nuragic holy wells) of a foyer, a descending stone staircase and an elliptical wall(tholos) wich encloses the source. The well water still runs through the extremely fine and tigh fit of the blocks during the winter and spring. The 25 steps are covered by a tholos style ceiling.

The one hectare archaeological site consists of a big and circular basalt hut, the so-called "capanna delle riunioni" (the hut where meetings took place) with a big stone seat inside. One-tower nuraghe is located in the south-west part, surrounded by several well-mantained huts which date back to different periods.

Orune: Su Tempiesu

Location: Middle-East Sardinia -Orune

Age: Nuragic Age- From the Bronze Age to the early Iron Age (XII-IX century b.C.)

If you want to disclose the mystery of the Sacred Wells you cannot miss the nuragic source "Su Tempiesu". Fortunately, this site has been perfectly preserved. Most of nuragic wells in the Island have only the well's structure and the stairs, whereas "Su Tempiesu", probably due to a landslide that protected it till 1953, keeps its original structure.

This beautiful well shows that the nuragic sources were really solid buildings. They were fascinating and cosy temples and probably only priest had access to them. The stones used for the nuragic wells are set with more accuracy than the ones used for the nuraghi.

Furthermore stone working is more regular and accurate. You can find this kind of building all over the Island, in Paulilatino, Bonorva or Olbia for instance. The holy source "Su Tempiesu" is the only one with a double roof due to the shale wall covering it. This temple was probably built at the end of the Bronze Age and it was used till the early Iron Age.

The fore part of the holy source, tre metres and half high, is formed by a triangular element ending with a pyramidal block.

The holy source Su Tempiesu is composed by trachyte and basalt stones connected to lead cramps. The stones used to build this monument may have been carried from far away because in the area around the temple there are only schist and granite outcrops. Many blocks have some particular juts (rustications) with a knoll shape. Their aim was probably to facilitate the transportation of the stones. But some reliable scientists, such as Lilliu and Taramelli, consider it nuragic symbols. According to this interpretation the knolls could represent the Mother Cult giver of water, life and nourishment.

Su Tempiesu follows the classical nuragic well's pattern, there is vestibule, a staircase (4 steps in this case) and a cell (with a "tholos" roof) to keep the source water. Also in this case the ground is made with trachyte blocks with a little round hollow used to purify the water. During the high-water, water spilling over the well flows off through an ingenious canal. In the first step there is a little gutter going on to a second source placed in the lower part of the monument. The archaeological finds have been found in this source during the excavations (they are today at the National Archaeological Museum of Nuoro).

Ozieri Town

Ozieri is a small town enjoying a propitious hilly location and overlooking a vast plain where man's work cohabits with a still uncontaminated nature. The environment, the monuments and architectural features of the historical centre of the city witness a culture which goes back to the Neolithic age, 5000 years ago was characterized by the important settlement of the Grotte di S. Michele (S. Michael's Caves) where were created the famous vases, remains of the "Ozieri Culture".

Archaeological Museum: The archaeological museum of Ozieri shows e rich collection of the most fascinating and suggestive finds in Ozieri's area.

Sospiri: The sweets of Ozieri are very much appreciated and sought after. So are in particular the famous Sospiri di Ozieri delicious candies of almond paste, honey, lemon covered with a thin icing and wrapped in coloured paper.

Spianata (thin bread): Known even beyond Sardinia as the Spianata di Ozieri (flat bread of Ozieri) it is an extremely ancient bread still unaltered. Always present on the tables of Logudoro both during daily meals and festive ones, it is also employed at work by farmers and shepherds because it keeps intact for many days its taste and fragrance. Even nowadays the modern bakeries make it with water, salt, yeast and the best flour of special wheat (semolato di grano). It is a bread which goes perfectly well with soups, salads, meats, milk or yogurt. Very handy for quick snacks as "puppias" (little dolls rolled up with sausage or cheese stuffing) it is also widely used as a sort of tray for roasted meat. It can be an excellent basic ingredient for traditional or revisited dishes.

Sa Greviera: The pastures of the Field of Ozieri has promoted throughout the centuries the breeding of mild cattle. During the Piemontese reign, cattle Bruno-Alpina breed were introduced into Sardinia and was also supported the production of cheese from cow-milk like the Greviere a cheese from the mountains. The typical ocellated (eye-like - occhiatura) spots of this cheese is due to the propionic bacterium still present and diffused throughout the plain of Ozieri. Once forgotten for decades the local Administration is now successfully attempting to relaunch it as a particular product (a product responding to a specific taste) Sa Greviera thanks to the genuineness of the milk it is made of, is very rich in demand for its typical taste, and it is appreciated both when young and when fully matured, and even as dressing for first courses.

Sassari City

Sassari is the second city for importance, politics and inhabitants (about 120000) in Sardinia. It is situated in the northern part, on a large calcareous tableland and its economy is mostly based on the tertiary sector. At the entrance of the city, coming from Alghero, there is the beautiful church of Santa Maria and it's monastery;

a bit further there are the public gardens and the palace of University. Not far there is the main square in Sassari, Piazza d'Italia, with the monument in honour of Vittorio Emanuele, Provincia and Giordano palace.

In via Roma there is the archaelogical museum "G. A. Sanna". In viale san Pietro there is the small church of San Pietro in Silky, a country church, now in the city, where the beloved statue of "Madonna delle Grazie" is kept. In the historic centre are gathered San Nicola Cathedral, Palazzo Ducale (XVIII century), the seat of the town council and the Santa Caterina church (XVI-XVII century), in late-Reinassance style. Not far from via Rosello you can see some ruins of the walls, the church of Trinità and the Rosello Funtain.

Sassari is more than art and history, is also wild nature and beautiful sea. About 15 kilometres far from Sassari, in Porto Torres direction, there is Platamona beach, a long seashore belonging to the commons of Sassari and Sorso. Platamona is, like Poetto Beach in Cagliari, Sassari's traditional beach; here you can find well equipped establishment.

The Nuraghis

Historical period: bronze age iron age (1800/1000 BC)
If the afterlife exists, probably an entire population observes Sardinia and smiles.

This population is the nuragic population which observes people who try to interpret the Tombs of the Giants, the nuragic wells, the holy sources and the nuraghi.

Sardinia counts at least 8000 ancient towers made with stones; in the past it was possible to count 20000 constructions like these. We wonder why this advanced, civil and powerful population used to spend time building towers. We wonder if their aim was religious, military or if they used to build these constructions in order to live there. Maybe we will not be able to give an answer to these questions and this is why it seems that the nuragic people laugh from the afterlife.

The nuraghi are unique. They are the biggest megalithic sights of Europe and most of them are also still well-preserved. The millennium have not solved all the doubts on the nuraghi's existence.

In Sardinia you can find a nuraghe every 3 kms so it is hard to believe that the towers belonged to powerful shepherds or to the normal people. It is not possible that many powerful shepherds could live so close to each other and it is not possible that there were only 20000 "houses" on the isle. The nuragic people probably lived in the huts near the nuragic "royal palaces".

Probably these tholos constructions were military fortresses. This is maybe the reason why nuragic people (probably associated to the Shardana) used to build many towers on impassable areas like the Sardinian hills or coasts; however, many experts say that, apart from the Barumini village, the nuraghi were not suitable from a military point of view.

The human being is fortunately an animal which does not give up easily. The nuragic doubts have not excited only the experts of archaeology but also simple lovers. Many theories have pushed the experts to study the nuraghi also according to the cyclical events of the vault of heaven like the sunrise and the sunset, the lunar cycle, the equinox, the solstice and the strange correspondences with the rising of the Centaur-Crux constellations.

Among the most convincing theories there is the idea that the nuraghi were places of mother cult. Their structure could represent a mother's womb with an opening that gives light, a light which could represent the man's fertilizing force. This is one of the possibilities that explain the orientation of many nuraghi with the entrance located on the South/South-East.

There are also other studies which confirm that The Shardana knew the megalithic yard: a unit of prehistoric measurement, used by the dolmen and megalithic circles builders.

There are several theories, all possible, probably because several were the uses of these constructions. Maybe the nuraghi were used like houses or religious sights, linked to the vault of heaven and the death cult, but also like military fortresses which allowed the nuragic people to sight the enemies

Torralba

The area of Torralba has been densely inhabited since the Nuragic Age, as testified by the nuraghe of Santu Antine. The medieval village, which rises around the monastery and the church of Santa Maria, owned by the Regno Giudicale of Porto Torres. We suggest you visit the archaeological and ethnographic museum of Torralba, that houses the archaeological heritage of the land, that thanks to its importance, is called "Valle dei Nuraghi" (Nuraghe valley).

The nuraghe of Torralba is the most famous and imposing of this area. Its name comes from San Costantino, the Roman emperor that was the main supporter of the Christian conversion of the island. The nuraghe rises on a huge plain, where there are many other nuraghi. The "reggia nuragica" (nuragic royal palace) is in the centre of a triangular bastion, with three minor towers located on the corners. The central tower has a diameter of 15 metres and half, it was more than 20 metres high (nowadays it is 17 metres high), and is built by 28 lines of basaltic stones. Inside you can admire the symmetry and the functionality utilized to make the best use of the space. Around the big central rooms, that were used for meetings and protective places, there are the passages, lit by slits equally distant one from the other.

Arzachena

Arzachena is situated 5 kilometres far from homonymous gulf and 25 from Olbia. The village, formerly under Tempio Pausania's administration, became autonomous municipality in 1922; nowadays it has become a well known summer resort but very rich in prehistoric monuments, too.

The centre of the town consists in a nicer square and Via Umberto, that ends with a flight of steps leading to the small church of Santa Maria Maggiore. In the outskirts you can see a curious granitic rock in the shape of mushroom, along the road that leads to Luogosanto, there is the Necropoli called "Li Muri", a typical example of a circular group grave. Near there is one of the most important and Bettener-preserved Tomba Dei Giganti in the island; going on alone the same way, there is another Giants Grave, "Coddu 'Ecchju" where a 15-metre-long and 4-metre-high granitic stone stands.

Among the Olbia-Palau road, about 2 kilometres far from Arzachena, there is one of the most interesting prehistoric monuments in this area: nuraghe Albucciu; not far from here, about 45 minutes on foot, there is the nuragic templed called Malchittu (1200 b. C.), a unique in its genre building, formed by an irregular hall and a large room where the ruins of a stony seat are situated.

Along the panoramic road towards Costa Smeralda, you will find, one after the other, four beatiful beaches: Cala di Volpe, Liscia Ruja, Long Beach and Capriccioli, all sheltered by a promontory called

Capriccioli and surrounded bu strawberry-trees and cistus plants. Yachts belonging to Italian and international jet set often frequent the surprisingly beautiful waters of this area.

Bonnanaro

The name of Bonnanaro, an inland town in the province of Sassari, is largely linked to the important historical discoveries that have been made in the area. The tomb that was found in 1889 at "Korona Montana" allowed the discoverers to identify numerous characteristics of the warrior population that lived at the dawn of the nuragic civilisation and started the so-called "culture of Bonnanaro"; many archaeological remains of weapons have come down to us as well as some pieces of pottery, which were used for burial purposes and were very austere with no trace of decoration.

The present day Bonnanaro grew up in the very heart of the Meilogu, on the slopes of Monte Pelao; it had an important strategic position for the ancient inhabitants of the island. It is a small centre (1,127 inhabitants) and the economy is based mainly on agriculture and sheep farming. A distinctive feature is the production of cherries; every year a cherry festival is held on the second Sunday in June. Wine is also produced very widely. It's well worth visiting the Sanctuary of the Madonna delle Grazie on Monte Arana, which has recently been restored.

The Sacred Wells

Historical period: end of bronze age-beginning of iron age (1500/900 BC)

The nuragic well is another important element of the Sardinian megalithic heritage. At the moment we can count 40 wells reachable thanks to a monumental staircase after which there is an atrium with the water.

This is a tholos room with a hole through which it is possible to look outside.

The nuragic wells are similar to the nuraghi's architectural structure but they have been built underground. The wells had many symbols. They represented the female sexual organs like if they were the entrance and the exit towards the afterworld.

The fact that the wells were full of water (the water reminds the amniotic fluid) let us think that the wells wanted to represent the womb of the mother earth.

The descent (or the climb) of the staircase represents the passage from the light to the darkness and viceversa. The water represents the birth.

These symbols explain the astronomical orientation of the holy wells. In the case of the sacred well of Santa Cristina in Paulilatino-Oristano, it has been assessed that thanks to the hole situated on the tholos vault, the moon is reflected on the well. This happens during a predefined period, that is to say at the utmost declination of the moon, every 18 years and 6 months. Thanks to the staircase, the sun's light is reflected in the well during the autumn equinox (between the 22nd and the 23rd of September) and also during the spring equinox (between the 20th and the 21st of March).

The moon's peculiarity has been noticed also in other wells; also the solar reflection is sometimes visible during the summer solstice (between the 20th and the 21st of June). Not all the wells have the tholos structure. There are also megaron temples with a rectangular plant with different spaces and with the sloping roof. According to the archaeological experts it is possible to compare these temples to the dwellings of the ancient Troia and Micene.

Oristano

The centre of the city is Arborea Square, where a monument in honour of Eleonora D'Arborea stands. Here are also grouped the main buildings of the city, like the Town Hall (XVII century), at first a monastery then houses the municipal offices. Going on towards the city centre you will find The Cathedral, the church of the Santissima Trinità, the Seminario Tridentino, the monastery of Carmelitani (XVIII-XIX century) and the church of san Francesco.

On the last Sunday and the last Tuesday of the Carnival in Oristano takes place the popular "Sa Sartiglia", an old relaxing horse race of the XVI century.

The museum of the Antiquarium Arborense houses a small art gallery where pictures, that date back to the Spanish domination, are kept, and exhibits various remains brought to light from the excavations of Tharrosand Sinis Peninsula. On the north of the

Oristano Gulf you will find Marina di Torregrande, the city seashore, that owns a well equipped tourist harbour. Here rises one of the most imposing Sardinian coastal towers, named "Sa Turri Manna", that overlooks Torregrande beach, traditional destination of city inhabitants.

Along the road that leads to Cuglieri you will find the beach of Is Arutas, with a sand composed by granules of quartz, followed by the beach of Is Arenas, where a rock modelled by the waters as an arch, named "S'Archittu" (the little arch), stands. A bit further on you will find the beach of Santa Caterina di Pittinuri

Ancient Town of Galtellì.

Treasures of the Ancient Town of Galtellì.
Set in enchanting surroundings and only a short distance from the amazing beaches of the Gulf of Orosei, Galtellì is a town steeped in history, rich in

religious art, architecture and tradition with the charm of a lifestyle that has become a rarity.

Worthy of an attentive visit are the churches. First and foremost the Romanic cathedral of San Pietro adorned with medieval frescoes that relate back to the Byzantine tradition and depict scenes from the old and new testament. Also of great artistic value are the polychrome wooden figures such as the 13th century Cristo Crocifisso (Christ on the Cross) created in the Tuscan gothic style and to which many miraculous acts have been attributed thus attracting devoted visitors from all over the island.

During Holy Week the whole community participates in what is an emotional and deeply moving experience. Led by the confraternity, a procession winds its way through the silent town accompanied only by the chants of the choir in this annual renewal of archaic devotional practices and rites.

Very appealing and worth a visit are the ruins of the medieval castle of Pontes, one time family residence of the Barons who presided over the area.

Throughout the entire territory are reminders of a long gone era evidence of which can be found on visiting the hypogeiche tombs or "Domos de Jana" some of which are situated within the residential part of the town. Even more attractive is the old centre of the town with its architecture and scenes of traditional everyday life. The townsfolk evoke the images, the environment, the houses, the essence, the silence and the spirit of the Galtellì described in Grazia Deledda's acclaimed novel "Canne al Vento" (Reeds in the Wind). It is still possible to catch a glimpse of the places that inspired the great masterpiece as many of them are still intact today. The Deleddian Literary Park is dedicated to this Nobel winning author.

The Ethnographic Museum in Via Garibaldi is still known locally as "Domos è sos Marras" (house of the Marras). This 17th century dwelling houses a collection that recounts and gives insight to the lifestyle, traditions and economy of a farming community over the centuries.

Galtellì takes pride in the significant number of hospitable places offering comfortable accommodation where visitors become temporary citizens and participants in savouring the essence and marvelling at the Galtellì of the celebrated novel "Canne al Vento" by Grazia Deledda.

In the town of Galtellì there are a large number of restaurants and accommodation facilities to choose and where guests will taste delicious flavours and will enjoy local traditions.

Olbia - Monti

The departure is from Olbia, probably one of the locations in Sardinia that has changed its name the most during the course of its history. Founded by the Punic people as a commercial landing around the fourth century A.C., it passed, like the rest of the Island, under Roman rule and acquired great importance during the Imperial age with its present name as a feud of the Julia family. History reveals that it was also patrimony of Atte, rich concubine of the Emperor Nerone. With the decline of Rome's supremacy, Olbia also declined, to relive again under the name of Fausiana and then, towards the year 1000, take on the name of Civita and then of Terranova, under the Ancient Kingdom of Gallura. It has another decline during the period of Spanish domination, to regain, with the intensification of traffic to Rome, capital of Italy, its important role as the port of access to Sardinia and the closest port to the Italian peninsula.

Situated in a profound bay, with a fertile, level inland, Olbia, with its port and airport, has reached a remarkable development thanks also to the numerous tourist resorts that extend, from North to South, along a coast of considerable beauty. The city is equipped with all types of facilities, hotel and restaurant structures making it extremely inviting. Interesting is the Romanic church of Saint Simplicio, built in granite hewn stone towards the end of the eleventh century. In its interior can be found a lovely collection of Roman funerary tombstone inscriptions. From Olbia you move on to the foot of the ragged Mount Limbara and the near artificial lake of Coghinas to reach Ozieri. A town with a suggestive appearance, constructed in the form of an amphitheatre in a sheltered basin, its architecture retains the aspect of "nobility", with its stone buildings ornate with colonnades.

It is one of the greatest dairy producers with sheep, cattle, and above all horse breeding farms. In the nearby Chilivani, there is a horse breeding centre and a racetrack for horse galloping races. The culinary traditions of the products of its countryside are excellent, and famous are the "suspiros" typical biscuits made of almond dough and wrapped in colorful paper. The town's cultural life is intense. It hosts the most prestigious literary award for poetry and prose in the Sardinian language.

Upon leaving Ozieri, on the S.S. 128, you reach Pattada, with its outskirts that are evocative both from a naturalistic and archaeological point of view. It is a centre famous for the production of the jack knives most used in Sardinia and probably, in all Italy, since the name "pattada" is commonly used to describe the hundreds of thousands of jack knives that are produced far from the Island. The authentic Pattada knife, that today is associated with the name of some great craftsmen, is an authentic jewel of quality blade production.

The knife doesn't have springs or locks, and presents itself in a characteristic lengthened leaf form to which a tempera flush is applied with a technique that is carefully kept secret and passed on from one generation of artisans to another. Upon leaving Pattada you move along the S.S. 389, that leads to Buddusò, a granite production centre, which presents itself in the grey shades of the stone that is used in the construction of all of the homes and pavements of the town. It is a sensation of almost uniform severity.

Buddusò is also the home of skilled craftsmen who work and carve wood. The object typically made by these artisans is a trunk. It is the most traditional and antique piece of furniture made by Sardinian wood craftsmen. At present the Sardinian trunks that expert artisans continue to produce have become very precious furniture elements. From Buddusò you proceed to the S.S. 389 to reach Monti. The landscape unfolds itself in a setting of incredible silence and rare, savage beauty. Cyclopean masses and granite pinnacles jut out from pastures that are broken here and there with small woods that get thicker as you go along, losing themselves in the horizon.

The streams that intersect the primitive landscape are deeply embanked and lost in little ravines, leaving uncovered the rounded rocks in its bed that contrast with the other granite rocks that are modeled by the wind with its flurry fantasy. Before reaching Monti, at the bottom of the valley, you can admire the scenario of the Mount Limbara with its ragged silhouette. The countryside around Monti is made up of well kept and orderly vineyards. This small and gracious town is dedicated to the cork industry and wine production.

The white wines of Monti are very well known, amongst which excels Vermentino, used also for desserts and as an aperitif. The local Social Bottle Cellar annually hosts (on the first Sunday in August) the well known Sagra di Vermentino (Festival of Vermentino). Upon leaving Monti you join a new road that leads directly and rapidly to Olbia.

Mamoiada

Situated just a few kilometres from Nuoro, Mamoiada (pop. 2,580) is a characteristic agricultural and sheep-farming village with beautiful woodland surroundings in an upland area. The area has a very rich archaeological heritage; it is reckoned that man has settled in the district of Mamoiada since the 15th century B.C., as we can see from the clear evidence confirming the existence of civilisations from the ancient past in the area. There are many nuraghi:

"Arràilo" in the area of "Sa Pruna", "Monte Juràdu" on the road to Orani, "Orguru" on the road to Fonni.

There are also some "domus de janas" dating back to the Neolithic-nuraghic period, including the notable group of six "domus" on the main Mamoiada-Fonni road, called "Sas Honchèddas de Istevène". One of the most important menhir is a certain granite statue, called "Sa Perda Pintà", dating back to the 3rd millennium B.C., whose carved niches and unusual concentric designs make it a unique example in Sardinia. In the village itself you can visit the Church of Nostra Signora di Loreto that probably dates back to the Middle Ages. One of the most interesting small country churches is the Sanctuary of the SS Cosma e Damiano, dating back to the 7th century and regarded as the oldest example in Barbagia.

Mamoiada's most popular attraction is undoubtedly its Carnival, one of the oldest traditional folk events in

Sardinia. The most characteristic costumes of the Carnival processions, that take place on the Sunday and Tuesday in carnival week, are the "Mamuthones" with their wooden masks; they parade through the village with rhythmic step, accompanied by the "Issohadores" dressed in red shirts and white trousers. The "Museo delle Maschere Mediterranee" (Museum of Mediterranean Costumes) is a particularly interesting place to visit, where they display the masks and costumes of Mamoiada and many others from all around the Mediterranean.

The People and Culture

Strong and proud Sardinian People

Sardinians are strong, proud, attached to land and tradition, small in number, not in spirit.

Long isolation and a past marked by foreign dominations and invasions have left them friendly, yet a bit cold. However, after a first impact, they turn into a hospitable and generous people. Thus, for example, primarily in hamlets, you are often invited immediately to an event like a birth or marriage or simply to taste special, home-made food.

Indeed, due to harsh life conditions, traditional Sardinia puts strong emphasis on rituality and ceremonies such as baptisms, engagements, illness-deaths, identified as the key steps of the "life cycle".

From Sacred to Profane

As in other Italian regions, Catholic faith is the predominant religion in Sardinia. There are many highly suggestive religious events such as Alghero's Holy Week and Saint Ephesus' Festival.

Besides these "religious rites", there are other popular festivals, historically and anthropologically important, marked by the cycle of an old agropastoral economy. Though recently influenced by tourism and technical innovation, such festivals remain genuine and are still reminiscent of the past.

Still visible are some elements belonging to the local prehistoric cultures, to the Classical and Byzantine heritage and, mainly, to the spectacular and choreographic Spanish religiosity in an extraordinary mix of sacred and profane.

Ream Mythical People

Sardinia: home of great men and women

From the literature to the music, from the politics to the cinema and arts, there are many important personality in the Sardinia's history, culture and social life. Grazia Deledda, Antonio Gramsci, Emilio Lussu, Paolo Fresu, Antonio Segni, Francesco Cossiga, Enrico Berlinguer, are only some of the numerous names that made Sardinia great and popular worldwide.

Eleonora d'Arborea and her "Carta de Logu"

Among the most rappresentative characters of Sardinian history, there is the female figure of Eleonora d'Arborea, mithical governor who inspired for ages numerous legends on her life and her conduct, for that she has been compared with the french Jeanne d'Arc. Married with the genoese Brancaleone Doria, she was the governor of Arborea "Giudicato" from 1383 till her death in 1404. She opposed all her forces to Aragonese powers, which aimed to occupied the island, and she was the promoter of different alliances and claims for the indipendence of Sardinia. But her fame is linked to the the law-code she had promulgated in the 1395 an called "Carta de Logu", written in sardinian language, and extended after to all Sardinia. This code rappresent one of the most civilized medieval juridical science.

Castello Giudicale Eleonora d'Arborea

The castle Eleonora d'Arborea is located in the village of Sanluri, in the province of Cagliari. The castle is opened to the public and is particularly interesting because it is one of the best-preserved Medieval fortresses in Sardinia. The castle itself is built on a regular, square plan and stands inside a fortress, which is enclosed by 1,550 m. of defence walls 4.5 metres high. 15 towers dominate the whole area, which covers 16 hectares, four of which stand guard at the entrances to the fortress.

Via Villa Santa, Sanluri (CA)

Ph. +39 070 9307105 - +39 070 9307184

Giuseppe Garibaldi: the "Lyon" of Caprera
Giuseppe Garibaldi reach for the first time Caprera the 25 of September 1849. There was all the population in "Cala Gavetta" to welcome the hero; everybody wanted to know the author of so many exploits in the world. It's been just in Caprera that Garibaldi matured his dream of Italy unit, with Rome as capital of the Kingdom. The following events belong to the great history but just a few know that after the historical meeting of "Teano" after having hand a kingdom of 9.000.000 people over to Vittorio Emanuele , Garibaldi came back to Caprera bringing with him three horses, one seeds sack and one stockfish bale. He was followed by a few friends and to be able to pay the cost of the his journey he had to borrow 3.000 lire.

Religious feasts and rural cults

Connected to the religious calendar of the Saints' festivals and summer cycle of agricultural crop, rural festivals stay vital in Sardinia. To celebrate a special event, people leave their own hamlet and go to old country churches.

The Sardinian tradition of rural cults gave rise, especially in internal areas and, often, in inaccessible and lonely places, to a typical architectural style. Pilgrims often stay in lollas, cumbessias, muristenes (small houses) near the church. Whole families with furnishings move to the villages-sanctuaries in order to spend the period of Novena, as well as socializing intensively with people. The organizers are responsible for rule compliance during the festivals: in fact, daily routine is suppressed, the convivial and exchange rites unite with the devotion for the saint invoked: tradition (namely, food, games, singing and dancing) clashes with mass culture.

For those who are eager to get acquainted with the Sardinian people's identity, its attachment to tradition and the desire to keep its own history and culture, attending these events is undoubtedly a unique experience. There are many (over 1000) antique celebrations.

Art and Archaeology
Origins - 6000 b.C TO 2500 b.C
The first artistic events in Sardinia date back to the ancient Neolithic age (6000-4000 BC). To this period belong the terracotta vase fragments decorated by impressing the valve of a seashell - the popular white arsella (clam) of Marceddì on raw clay. Between 4000 and 2500 BC the Culture of Bonu Ighinu developed in the island, with small urban settlements and finely

decorated ceramics in addition to the Culture of Ozieri, which saw the enlargement of towns and development of funerary architecture. Indeed, there is significant proof of archaic cults connected to the "Great Mother Land", "Fertile sky" and "Cult of the Dead". The domus de janas (fairy homes), rock tombs formed by an antechamber with wall niches and a chamber facing cells for the dead, belong to this period, too. Also important is St. Andrea Priu Necropolis, at Bonorva, some 50 km from Sassari, NE, on a 10-m-high trachyte wall with 20 domus de janas.

Nuragic Civilization - 2500-1500 BC

Megalitism spread on the island from 2500-1800 BC, with dolmen - simple burial chambers made of massive upright stones set into the ground and covered by a capstone and by perdas fittas (pierced stones), monoliths forming a circle that often bordered the tombs. In the Copper Age, Filigosa and Abealzu replaced the Ozieri culture. Towards the 16th century, the nuragic civilization developed, leaving 8000 nuraghes behind; the latter is a megalithic construction with one or more towers, interconnected with each other between galleries and ring-like corridors, with central aisle, pointed arch, defensive terraces and brackets. Nuraghes were placed in strategic points, often connected with each other, as can be seen visiting the Valle dei Nuraghi at Torralba (NW).

Usually, near Nuraghi there are the Giants' Tombs, collective megalithic burial places formed by a corridor covered with exedras and bordered by smooth plates, with central monolithic stele and doorway called "delle anime" stand. This structure can still be seen when visiting, for instance, the Giants' tombs of "Lu coddu ecchju" (or Capichera), 14 m long, and surmounted by a 4-m granite stele and that of "Li Lolghi" both nearby Arzachena (NE).

The nuraghe civilization is still visible in the Monteclaro and BonnanaroCultures, characterized by the processing of metals from which the numerous small bronzes found on the island, statues portraying warriors, ships and animals, were forged. The cult of water was evidence of religious faith and in its honor well temples or sacred wells were raised: these constructions feature ceiling stairs down to the level of groundwater (wells) under a false dome structure. The construction technique is more refined than that used for nuraghes, as witnessed by the sacred well of Santa Cristina in the province of Oristano (NW).

Phoenicians and Romans in Sardinia

Phoenicians invasions started in VIII century BC: this brought the first colonies along the coast: Bithia (Chia), Tharros, Nora, Carales. Still visible in these centers are signs of this ancient civilization and subsequent domination (Roman domination) under which they expanded further and flourished. Nora excavations show baths, floor mosaics, a beautiful II-cent. BC theatre, while two temples built around a "Punic" plant and two thermal structures, in addition to the remains of the ancient city, were found in Tharros.

With the Middle Ages and the intensification of commercial relations with the Maritime Republic of Pisa, Romanic art developed in Sardinia. The latter is the most important and varied in architecture. Most churches date from the XII to XIII centuries. Even though most churches are very different from one another, one can identify common traits such as the use of different stones, usually red trachyte and the use of different colors for the facades. Note Olbia's St. Simplicio cathedral and St. Saccargia Trinity Church. Worth visiting are also older churches like S. Giovanni di Sinis (built around the XI century). After the Aragonese came the Pisans who left traces, instead, of a Gothic-Baroque style as witnessed by the Cathedral and the church of St Mary of Bethlehem in Sassari.

Ancient Arts and Crafts

The society revolves around the land, as evidenced by the presence of shepherds and farmers, the two main trades in the traditional sardinian world. Such occupations were not theoretically learned, but acquired from experience and long-matured cultural heritage, generating two different contrasting life styles.

Another key occupation in Sardinian society is the artisan, because the latter produces tools and equipment for peasant, pastoral and domestic work. Presently, this job has been highly revaluated, because its products are highly attractive during summer local fairs.

Farm-holding goods like equipment and saddles are augmented by typically feminine things like embroidery, weaving, baskets, packaging of bread and pastries, or particularly precious gold and leather objects - now also famous abroad and highly valued.

Travel Information Guide
Discover the island

Sardinia: a wonderful land

In Sardinia is possible to enjoy a holiday in lots and different ways. The geological nature of the territory, its climate and geographic position make Sardinia a special and unique place.

Everyone arriving in Sardinia for the first time has the feeling of entering another world consisting of endless spaces and majestic landscapes.

Surrounded by the sea, Sardinia, in fact, features a unique, unmatched territory.

The island, due to its insular position and historical

events, is one of the Mediterranean areas where popular traditions are less contaminated by the outside world.

Just think of the fascinating domus de janas, the origin of nuraghes or tombe dei giganti (the giants' tombs), the Sacred Wells, the mysterious menhir dating back to the Bronze Age, in addition to a heritage characterized by ethnomusical traditions, poetry and literature in the Sardinian language.

4 GOOD REASONS TO FLY TO SARDINIA

1. **Low cost flight to Sardinia**

More sun, saving money.

Meridiana, AirBerlin, Easy Jet, Jet2.com, Norwegian, Air Baltic, Vueling, Volotea, Germanwings, Transavia and many more...all of them offer a large ammount every day of discounted flights from most important european cities. Thanks to the low cost companies, the concept of distance change and Sardinia become more accessible even just for the week-end. Flight, accomodation, tipical food, drinks, a juice of holiday for everyone.

2. The deepest canyon in Europe

In Barbagia area, in the east-centre of Sardinia, dipped in the spectacular Supramonte, surrounded by thick forest and splendid oleanders, we can find the most impressive natural abyss of Europe: "Su Gorroppu" gorge, also called Gran Canyon of Europe. This is one of the fascinating and impressing simbol of Gennargentu Mountains.

The height of the huge vertical faces exceed 400 meters. The gorge is a deep wound of calcareous rocks sculpted by water and shaped during the millenniums courses by the rio Flumineddu rushing water, between Orgosolo Supramonte and Urzulei mountain; the river continue his course over the canyon , creating numerous small lakes and going down to Dorgali valley where it feed different sources.

3. The highest dunes in Europe

One of the less known area in Sardinia, but not for that less interesting, is the western south coast of the island, where we can find the primary dunes complex, which beuaty is extended in the territory of Arbus, Guspini and Gonnosfanadiga towns.

Piscinas is one of the most important natural environment on regional, national and mediterranean scale. Dunes have a strong landscape effect that leaves visitors breathless.

The beach is about 6 km. long with 50 meters high dunes, plenty of blooming asphodels.

Piscinas and the nearby Arcuentu mountain are in Arbus area, in the province of Cagliari.

4. The widest museum opened to the sky in the world

Sardinia could be rightly considered, the biggest open

sky museum in the world, with his 7.000 Nuraghi, misterous solidly stone-made construction, that for theirs architectural peculiarity can be assimilated to pyramids, scattered evrerywhere in the region; the big megalithic monuments formed by Dolmen, Giants'Tombs, sacred wells, Domus de janas, rappresent the tipical elements of civility of the nuraghi, that make sardinia unique in the planet.

Tourist Attraction

The archipelago of La Maddalena, lies not far off the extreme northeastern coast of Sardinia. It is made up of four main islands, La Maddalena, Santo Stefano, Caprera and Spargi, situated near the Gallura's coastline and another three to the north, Budelli, Razzoli and Santa Maria, in the southern part of the straits of Bonifacio, surrounded by many rocks and numerous islets. All of granite, these islands are enchanting thanks to the rocks, the beaches and the sea.

La Maddalena is the biggest island of the Archipelago (19.061 s. km.). It is the only one of the seven islands to host a stable population. The higher hill, Guardia Vecchia, is not over 156 metres of height. The land, an undulating plateau with granite outcrops, does not afford cultivation and is mainly covered with low Mediterranean bushes.

Since 1996, it has been a National Park to safeguard the rare flora and fauna that still populate the islands. The flora is the typical Mediterranean one and is composed by 750 kinds of plants, like strawberry, "lentischio" (mastic tree), myrtle and rosemary but also pinewood, holm oaks and juniper bushes. In the park numerous rare specimen of lifebird nest, like the storm's bird, the cormorant and the Corsican gull. Particularly rich is the underwater life that can boast of the presence of the red encrusting seaweed, Lithophyllum lechenoides (very rare and protected), and of the huge Patella ferruginea.

Caprera is the second biggest island of the Archipelago. It is found to the east of La Maddalena. From the summit of Monte Telaione, reachable by a granite stairway, you can admire an extraordinary panorama of the whole island, as far as the northeastern coast of Sardinia and Santa Teresa di Gallura. Still unpopulated, frequented by only a few migrant shepherds from the 18th century, it was bought by Giuseppe Garibaldi in 1856, who lived there for long intervals, and died there in 1882. The house and the other buildings of Garibaldi's, are nowadays used as a museum, called "Compendio Garibaldino". Freed from an almost complete military occupation, it was declared, in 1982, a nature reserve. At Caprera, there is the tourist village of Club Méditerranée and a Sailing Centre of the Touring Club Italiano.

Between Palau and La Maddalena is found Santo Stefano, from where Napoleon shelled La Maddalena island in 1793. A few kilometres after, you find Spargi, with a circular form, surrounded eastward by a thin white sandy beach, that someone named "Boomerang". It's the most rich in water and vegetation. Northwards, there are the islands of Budelli, (well known for the Spiaggia Rosa (pink beach) wonderful scenery of an Antonioni's film, nowadays forbidden to visitors), Razzoli, accessible only from the west part, and Santa Maria with flat and fertile ground.

Protected Marine Areas

Discover the Marine Reserve of Sardinia: a huge variety of depth and colours concentrated in the wonderful protected marine areas that make Sardinia an island unique in the world...

Tavolara - Punta Coda Cavallo Park

Another pearl among sardinian parks is the "Isola di Tavolara" and "Capo Coda Cavallo" marine reserve. The reserve consists also in the minor Molara and Molarotto islands, made of granite covered with limestone cliffs, where the blue lizard lives. The fauna is extremely rich, some years ago among the various species it was possible to notice the sea monk . Marvellous is the expance of sea in the west coast of Molara named "piscine di Molara" (molara pool), for its colour and its transparent sea bed.

www.parks.it/riserva.marina.tavolara/

www.tavolara.it

Sinis-Isola di Mal di Ventre protected marine riserve

The Sinis Peninsula-Isola di Mal di Ventre (in the province of Oristano) is also a protected area, which

the ornithological significance of the ecosystem is so important that is considerate "humid zone of international relevance" by Ramsar Agreement in 1971. This coast border, with his historical patrimony (Tharros ruins, coastal town founded by Phoenicians), cultural and landscape richness (Is Arutas and Mari Ermi, beautiful beaches constitute by crystal quartz grains) is one of the most attractive region of Sardinia.
www.areamarinasinis.it/
www.parks.it/riserva.marina.penisola.sinis/

The Regional park and the protected Marine Area of Porto Conte e Capo Caccia-Isola Piana

The Regional park and the protected Marine Area of Porto Conte e Capo Caccia-Isola Piana are entirely included in the Alghero territory The Porto Conte Gulf (" Nimphaea natural harbour" of Romans) is characterized by impassable and inaccessible tracts. It preserved an important flora and fauna patrimony. The calcareous formations, specially constituted by cliffs, are the largest widespread karstification of emerged and submerged cavities in the Mediterranean. Among them, the "Nettuno" Cavity, 2500 meters long, made suggestive and famous all over the world for the salad lake it winds along inside.

www.ampcapocaccia.it/

The protected Marine Area of Capo Carbonara-Villasimius

The protected Marine Area of Capo Carbonara and the two islands of Cavoli and Serpentara just in front of it, represent a magnificent and unique natural park in the south-east Sardinia. The variety and original form of granitic rocks give particular nuances to the landscape. The small village of Carbonara which has become Villasimius, only in the 1862, takes its name from the intensive exploitation of charcoal practiced a long time ago. The submerged lands of Villasimius enclose archaeological finds of every ages relegate there for centuries from the numerous shipwrecked, the most ancient one is a Roman boat dated back to 250 A.C. that it was transporting a shiploade of medieval crockery.

www.ampcapocarbonara.it/

The Natural Parks

Discover the national parks in Sardinia. Wild nature and hidden paths... Natural parks where unique and beautiful animal species live. Such as the popular white donkeys in the Asinara Park in the North of the island or the pink flammingos in the South.

To find out where our parks are, from the north to the south of Sardinia click below:

North Sardinia

The Parks in The North of Sardinia

The national Park of Asinara

One of the last to be created (28th november 1997), the National Marine Reserve (in the province of Sassari, northwestern coast) is characterized by an extremely wild nature, due to the fact that no agricolture has ever been implemented here. In the next century the island was a jail of maximum security. The marine habitat is gorgeous and one of the most fascinating thing of the reserve is the marvellous fauna, with the "asino bianco" a tipical donkey species of the island. Wonderful beaches are widespread along all the cost, with cristal and pure water.

www.parcoasinara.it

www.parks.it/parco.nazionale.asinara/

Arcipelago della Maddalena National Park

The park is situated in the north-east of Sardinia and not only includes the homonymous isle but six minor islands too, Caprera, Santo Stefano, Spargi, Budelli, Santa Maria e Razzoli. It's considered, by many people,

for its colours, one of the most beautiful marine scenery in the world. Particularly coloured is the expanse of sea between the islands of Budelli, Santa Maria and Razzoli, which is the point where we observe seven shades of blue and for that called "Porto della Madonna". A boat trip is absolutely a must, specially by sailing-boat, during that it's not unusual to run into and followed by a group of young dolphins.
www.lamaddalenapark.it/
www.parks.it/parco.nazionale.arcip.maddalena/

The Regional park and the protected Marine Area of Porto Conte e Capo Caccia-Isola Piana

The Regional park and the protected Marine Area of Porto Conte e Capo Caccia-Isola Piana are entirely included in the Alghero territory The Porto Conte Gulf (" Nimphaea natural harbour" of Romans) is characterized by impassable and inaccessible tracts. It preserved an important flora and fauna patrimony. The

calcareous formations, specially constituted by cliffs, are the largest widespread karstification of emerged and submerged cavities in the Mediterranean. Among them, the "Nettuno" Cavity, 2500 meters long, made suggestive and famous all over the world for the salad lake it winds along inside.
www.ampcapocaccia.it/

Limbara Mountain Park
The Limbara represents the major massif of granitic origin in Sardinia. And it is just the characteristic of the granitic rock that creates a big variety of forms, strange incisions and boulder falls laid upon in a precarious balance (Sa Pedra Subrapare). The park can be considered a unique landscape due to its self-vegetation that at this time presents tree formations that constitute true relict as the yew " Taxus baccata" and the holly "Ilex aquifolium". Further more it is not difficult to observe a rare endemic specie as the

"Peonia Selvatica" with splendid colors. The park is also famous because it is very rich in water springs, fed by a very deep water circulation, renowned for the lightness of water.

www.sitos.regione.sardegna.it/nur_on_line/parchi/Limbara.htm

Centre of Sardinia

The Parks in the Center of Sardinia

Marghine-Goceano Park

The Marghine-Goceano Park is situated in the territory of 14 towns, among them Pattada and Macomer, and located exactly in the centre of Sardinia, between Siniscola coast and Bosa coast. Includes the Marghine mountain range (Punta Palai 1200 m.), the one of Goceano (Monte Rasu, 1259 m.) and the upland of Campeda (Monte Pedra Lada, 684 m.). The forestal patrimony of primary relevance in the regional scale is for the main part managed by Ente Foreste della

Sardegna. Among the most significant places are Badde Salighes Forest with autochthonous flora and exotic plants bedded in the middle of XIX century by the English engineer Benjamin Piercy. Of national interest is the Taxus forest (taxus baccata L.), which is the most wide of Sardinia and characterized by numerous centuries-old specimen.

www.goceano.it

Sinis-Montiferru Park

It is formed by the major volcanic massif of the island called "Montiferru" (700 kmq), Sinis peninsula and the Oristano plain. As well as the Urtigu Mountain (1050 m.) and a large-sized woody expanse, also the coastal stretch presents a remarkable fascination with its calcareous rocks shaped by the erosive action of the sea and wind, giving live to original forms and among these the most famous "Arco" of Santa Caterina di Pittinuri (S'Archittu), destination of numerous tourists and set of international happenings. Going down to the south towards Sinis peninsula we find instead one of the largest pinewood characterized by maritime pine in Italy.

www.sitos.regione.sardegna.it/nur_on_line/parchi/montiferru.htm

Giara of Gesturi
The park is an upland situated in the province of Oristano, between "Monte Arci" and Sarcidano region. It's famous all over the world for its wild beauty and for the presence of the unique Italian and European drove wild horses, well-known as "cavallini della Giara", with a distinctive almond-shaped eyes. The upland has been inhabited since the Neolithic age and later than occupied by nuragic people, fortifying the zone with 23 "Nuraghi" disposed on the edge of the tableland as points of observation and defence. Among them the protonuragic village of "Bruncu Madagui"

dated back to 1820 A.C. and considered the ancestor of all nuragic constructions.

Arci Mountain

Arci massif is one of the four volcanic formation of the island (Montiferru, Arcuentu, "Giara di Gesturi") dated back to 12-0,01 milions of years. The lavic bastion, which signs the upland border is remarkable with verticalities that can reach 60 meters. All the park area is marked by rich Ossidiana deposits, one kind of vitreous rocks generally black, that have made "Monte Arci" the most ancient ore district of the island. This Ossidiana has been the point of reference during the Neolithic age for Sardinia population and a big part of Mediterranean area . Infact it was used both for arrows and for lances, scrapers and knives.

www.sitos.regione.sardegna.it/nur_on_line/parchi/montearci_gal4.htm

South Sardinia

The Parks in the South of Sardinia
Monte Linas-Marganai-Oridda-Montimannu Park
Located in the south-west area of Sardinia, among urban centre of Villacidro in the north and the Iglesias towns in the south, this park is specially known for his granitic-schistose rise of "Monte Linas" (Perda de Sa Mesa, peak 1236 m.). As interesting is the most high permanent waterfall in Sardinia (the jump is about 50 Meters), formed by the Muru Mannu watercourse at the confluence with Linas stream. The "leccio" woods in the Montimannu and Marganai massifs are quite wide an particularly beauty, the last one is the unique in the south to be lay down in a calcareous rock substratum. And it is just for this land characteristic that the territory of this park is particularly reach in underground cavities. One of this is the impressive "Grotta di San Giovanni" (Domusnovas), stated "natural monument" by the Sardinian Region. In this cavity lives the Sardinian Geotritone, very interesting

cavernicolous amphibious. The park is also industrial archaeology: this angle has been the most interesting ore district of the island and all Italy.
http://www.sitos.regione.sardegna.it/nur_on_line/parchi/linas.htm

Sulcis Park
It is the most extensive regional park and it's situated along the south-west part of Sardinia. It presents a huge amazing landscapes variety such as the granitic rises of Monte Lattias, the calcareous ridges of Monte Tamara, the deep slopes of Is Pauceris valleys, the cliffs and the rock peaks of Conca D'Oru. But the most famous zone is the WWF Monte Arcosu-Monte Lattias Natural Reserve.

Sette Fratelli-Monte Genis Regional Park
It includes in his area almost all the Sarrabus region in the south-east of Sardinia. The granitic massif of Sette Fratelli (1023 m.), which has taken its name from the

main ridge seven tops, enclose marvellous landscapes as the incredible "Arco dell'Angelo" gorge and picturesque river valleys in the rocks. During the nineteenth century the place healthiness attracted numerous habitants of the nearby Cagliari (San Gregorio-Burcei settlement) and at the same time the presence in the country of important argentiferous vein brought to new activities and mine centres (Tuviois, Serra s'Ilixi Burchi, and more), which ruins are included in the N° 7 area of the Geomining Sardinia Park.

www.montesettefratelli.com

www.sitos.regione.sardegna.it/nur_on_line/parchi/settefratelli.htm

Molentargius - Saline Regional Park

The naturalistic zone and industrial-archaeological area of Molentargius-Saline is included in the towns lands of Cagliari, Quartu S'Elena, Quartucciu and Selargius. The symbol of this area is the famouspink flamingo, called by Sardinian people "genti arrubia" (red people) or Mangoni. They regularly winter in the Bellarosa basin. In this area it lives also "Cavaliere d'Italia", with one of the most important population in Europe. The park is not only fauna but industrial-archeology too, with the salt extraction activity of Poetto, which has held in the history, from Punic age to 1984, an important sector of the towns economy. This activity has had a qualitative influence on the environment and landscape (the Molentargius has taken its name by the donkey, that it was called in Sardinian language Molenti, used for salt transport).

www.apmolentargius.it/

Beaches in Sardinia

Sardinia's spectacular coastline boasts endless bays and coves with white sand beaches and crystal-clear emerald water. The island's beaches are genuinely some of the best the Mediterranean has to offer.

It is beautifully varied with dramatic limestone mountains dropping to secluded coves in the east, sand dunes in the west and glorious beaches to the north and south, most with gently shelving shorelines and shallow waters - perfect for all ages, including young children.

The beaches in Sardinia are incredibly clean and whether you're in one of the secluded bays or on one of the busier town beaches you will always find a very good standard of cleanliness - both in terms of the beach itself and in the quality of the water.

A good range of water sports is available on most coasts during summer, including waterskiing and windsurfing. Porto Pollo, near Palau in the north is a favourite spot for surfers and also the place for kite-surfing. Sailing is another popular pursuit, particularly around Alghero, the Costa del Sud, the Costa Smeralda and the Maddalena archipelago, however most will have to make do with joining a group with a full crew. Sardinia is also one of the Mediterranean's best locations for diving and there are local outfits offering tuition and excursions with full equipment provided.

Rather than give a long list of beaches we have broken them down into regions - just click on the links to select your choice. Please be aware that this is far from exhaustive, we've just tried to give a flavour of the breathtaking beaches Sardinia has to offer.

Costa Smeralda & North East
Beaches, Sports & Activities

The north east coastline of Sardinia offers a wealth of dazzling beaches with a mix of hidden coves and popular haunts. It also offers a feast of water sports with the Isola dei Gabbiani particularly popular.

Beaches

Santa Teresa

Enjoy stunning views of the straits of Bonifacio over the transparent turquoise sea as you head to the dramatic headland of Capo Testa to the west of Santa Teresa. The nearby bay of Santa Reparata has some delightful stretches of beach. To the east there are many small beaches around Porto Rafael and Palau.

Arzachena

This area is home to an array of attractive sandy beaches, some with a deep green backdrop of pine trees. To the north of Cannigione and Laconia you will find lots of sandy coves.

Tanca Manna sits approximately 250 metres from the road behind a saltwater lake. It has a great stretch of sand and plenty of facilities for families. A kilometre beyond Tanca Manna is Barca Bruciata, a small sandy beach which is quiet with no facilities.

Cala Capra beach just beyond Golfo delle Saline is a pretty sandy bay tucked beneath the impressive Capo D'Orso headland with its distinctive bear shaped weathered rock.

Costa Smeralda

There are many fantastic bays and beaches on the Costa Smeralda, some well signposted, others hidden down small, winding tracks. You will often find that the sea is behind a group of private villas, or that the only visible sign of a beach is a row of parked cars by the side of the road. In these cases it pays to leave the car and do a bit of exploring by foot. Our favourites include:

- The Capriccioli headland has five beautiful small sandy beaches. There are facilities for boat hire and also a bar close to the beach. These beaches, including La Celvia, are amongst the most popular in the area.

- Just before the Hotel Cala di Volpe is the beautiful Liscia Ruia, an extensive sweep of white sand set down a long unsurfaced road.

- Rather off the beaten track is the Spiaggia del Principe which cannot be reached by car. The last stretch has to be done on foot takes under 10 minutes and is well worth the effort.

- Piccolo Pevero is a small sandy beach with parasol and boat hire. It also has a restaurant ("Il Pulcino") and a bar.

- The Pitrizza beach at Liscia di Vacca just north of Porto Cervo is also popular.

San Teodoro

The main beach here is La Cinta which stretches north from the town with 5km of glistening white sand. This is a very popular beach, especially in July and August so be warned. There are plenty of facilities at this beach including water sports activities and snack bars.

If you are looking for something less busy, head for Capo Coda Cavallo. The larger beaches here have some facilities in high season but this headland is well worth exploring as there are many hidden coves undiscovered by the masses.

Another two we recommend are south of Olbia, Punta Molara and Cala Girgolu.

Sports & Activities

The Isola dei Gabbiani is particularly famous for its windsurfing conditions and attracts many enthusiasts each year.

Another great place for water sports is Cannigione. Here you will find a water sports centre where you can arrange windsurfing, sailing, water-skiing and fishing. There are a couple of other sailing schools in this area too. At the main mooring you are able to pick up small engine powered dinghies for day trips to the Maddalena Islands. Please note these are only suitable for experienced seafarers.

Cala di Volpe beach on the way to Capriccioli rents out dinghies, pedalos and windsurfs as well as offering some reputable dive centres.

Horse riding is very popular in this area. Schools can organise excursions in the countryside and rides along the beach. The best time of day to go is early in the morning and at sunset, most schools will be closed during the hottest part of the day.

Alghero & North West

Beaches, Sports & Activities

There is a fine choice of beaches northwards from the town of Alghero. During the summer months it is easy to find facilities for water sports to indulge in.

The Maria Pia beach, still in Alghero is a beautiful sandy bay backed by pinewoods. More beaches are to be found as you journey further around the bay of Alghero and around Porto Conte bay and beyond it. On the way to Porto Conte, just past Fertilia, try the beaches of Lazzaretto with superb views across to Capo Caccia and Le Bombarde, a strip of pure white sand bordered by crystal clear sea.

Beyond the headland of Capo Caccia there is a lovely long beach at Porto Ferro. Stintino, the north-western point of the island, has some fantastic beaches, including the almost tropical Pelosa.

To the south towards Bosa, the coastline tends to be more wild and rocky a paradise for snorkellers and scuba divers. There are a couple of sandy beaches including La Speranza which lies about eight kilometres south of Alghero.

Sports & Activities
Most beaches will have windsurfing boards and pedalos to rent. At the main port, as well as along the Lido, you will find companies which hire out small boats. There are diving schools here; past clients have used "Blue Services" and been very happy with the service they received.

In the summer months, horse and cart tours are available in Alghero, taking you on an hour long trip around the old town. It is a great way to see the sights and children love it. Tours start on the port side of Bastione della Maddalena where you will find the carriages waiting.

Southern Sardinia

Beaches, Sports & Activities

The Sulcis Iglesiente in the south west boasts 200km of coastline and the Sarrabus region in the south east another 200km. Both have a grand choice of magnificent beaches.

Beaches

Compared to other parts of the island, the south west coast is relatively underdeveloped whereas the south east coast is more developed and dotted with summer residential areas. However, with a little exploration you will find deserted bays and coves. The most popular beaches can be accessed by car followed by a short walk. Beware of the Mistral Wind; children's inflatable toys should not be used as the northerly wind will blow them out to sea….towards Tunisia!

Nora beach is a pleasant sandy beach which extends south of the Roman ruins of Nora. A popular destination for the townsfolk of Pula. It can be crowded during the hottest months. St Margherita is a long sandy beach which encompasses the summer resort of Forte Village Hotel and Abamar Hotel. Beach facilities are good here if you want to hire a speed boat or a sea scooter.

Chia is a dazzling beach and is perfect for those who love long sandy beaches. This idyllic beach, recently voted the 5th best destination for a beach holiday in Europe, has fine sand and is fringed with sand dunes. There is a growing number of ice cream booths which have appeared over the years where you are able to buy refreshments. Unfortunately this is a beach to avoid when the mistral wind blows as the sand is swept across the beach at very high speed and can be quite painful! There are facilities here to hire windsurfs and sea kayaks.

There are plenty of opportunities to partake in a spot of snorkelling if you wish to catch a glimpse of life beneath the sea. Cala Cipolla, Sa Tuerredda and Is Molentes beaches are perfect for this.

Amongst the most beautiful beaches of the Carbonara Gulf are towards Villasimius: Porto Sa Ruxi, Cala Piscadeddus, Campus or Foxi, Campulongu Beach, Spiaggia del Riso.

Sports & Activities

Choose from the many water sports including windsurfing, sea kayaking, sailing or scuba diving which can be organised from most beaches. Speedboats and sea scooters are also available to hire at some beaches so bear this in mind if you are looking for a peaceful spot to relax.

Bluefan Water Park is a fantastic day out for the children with a great selection of waterslides as well as other facilities including bars, restaurant and picnic area. It is located on the way to Cagliari.

If you wish to explore the lesser-known parts of the Sardinian mountains or along coastal trails, walks and climbs can be arranged to satisfy your own tastes and level of fitness. Sunrise and sunset walks are amongst the most popular requests. Also, gentle cycling or mountain hiking is a great way to cover longer distances and explore higher ground. Bike hire can also be arranged.

Fishing and horse riding are other popular activities in the area and can be arranged through several operators in the main tourist areas.

Getting Around

Hiring a car is the best way to get out and about, giving you the freedom to explore the island at your leisure, but there are trains across the island and a bus service.

By car, it only takes a few minutes to escape from the tourist routes into the untouched countryside, either along the spectacular coastline or in the mountains. Often you will have the road to yourself, and the island is rich in prehistoric archaeological sites which are well worth a visit.

Most of our self-catering properties are located in the countryside, a few kilometres away from beaches and main towns, it is therefore essential to have a car. Car hire is in great demand in July and August and not all car hire grades are available and so it is advisable to pre-book early.

Trains
The island's rail network connects into all the major towns on the island, however much of the east and centre of the island is not well served by trains. Alternatively, the "Trenino Verde", an old-fashioned steam train running various routes throughout the island during the summer months, offers a delightful way to discover Sardinia.

Tickets can be purchased at stations, through travel agents and online at www.trenitalia.it.

Bus

Most towns and villages are served by a network of buses, some beaches can also be reached by bus. Timetables however are not always adhered to and service on a Sunday tends to be somewhat restricted. Tickets should usually be purchased before boarding and are sold from ticket offices and local bars, but if that fails you can pay when you board. Buses around cities are an affordable way of sightseeing.

Cars

As mentioned previously car hire probably affords the most convenient way of travelling around the island. There are no motorways on Sardinia, but on the upside there are no toll roads either. Dual carriageways or superstradas run between most of the main cities, the main roads are generally good, the minor roads tend to be narrow and bendy, but as a consequence offer some spectacular scenery.

Please drive very carefully, especially at first, as it may take you some time before you feel comfortable driving in Sardinia. Extra care will need to be taken for guests staying in properties accessed by an unmade road. It is not unknown to encounter cows, pigs or other animals in the middle of the road so stay alert, especially at night when they are not readily visible. Drive well on the right hand side, remembering that minor, narrow roads may be unmarked but are still two-way. Bridges are often single lanes.

Remember that when rain occurs after a long dry period, the roads can become extremely slippery so always exercise caution. Unless otherwise indicated, a speed limit of 50km/h applies in built up areas. Outside built up areas and on single carriageway main roads, speed limits are 90km/h (80km/h in wet conditions) and on the few dual carriageways on the island, 110km/h (80km/h in wet conditions).

Places

Cagliari

Picturesque historical districts with sea views, elegant shopping streets and panoramic terraces, including the bastione di Santa Croce, a great place for a romantic evening after a fiery sunset. Cagliari is Sardinia's main and most populous city, at the centre of an urban area that counts 430,000 inhabitants (150,000 of them in the capital city alone) as well as the island's gateway port and main Mediterranean cruise liner hub. The city's history goes back thousands of years, from pre-historic times to the reign of the Savoy.

The Castello quarter sits perched on its highest hill and boasts ancient bastions that today are the heart and soul of nightlife, and picturesque streets lined by grand old homes: Palazzo Regio and Palazzo di Città, as well as the Cathedral of Santa Maria. The medieval towers - dell'Elefante and San Pancrazio - that stand guard at the entrance to the castle are well worth notice. Villanova connects to the Castle quarter via the stairway of the bastione di Saint Remy.

A passionate air of religious devotion takes over the quarter every year at Easter, during Holy Week, while during the rest of the year the elegant boutiques and churches welcome you with somewhat less ado: the cloister of San Domenico, the Church of San Saturnio, and the Basilica di Nostra Signora di Bonaria, the Christian temple of Sardinia. Below Castello you'll find the Marina quarter, which will impress you with lovely buildings and the porticos of Via Roma, including the Palazzo Civico.

Settled as a village of fishermen and merchants, it is the symbol of the town's multi-ethnicity. Here you will find the Church of Sant'Eulalia, home to precious remains from the Roman era. The Stampace quarter is the venue of the colourful yearly festival of Sant'Efisio in May, an event the entire island enjoys. Its narrow streets are home to the baroque Church of Sant'Anna. Don't forget to visit the nearby Anfiteatro, one of Sardinia's most important Roman ruins, and the Botanical gardens, a green oasis in the city's centre.

Just outside of town is the Castle of San Michele and Tuvixeddu, the Mediterranean's largest Phoenician-Punic necropolis (VI-III century BCE). When you are ready to surround yourself with nature, you can head towards a thousand different natural attractions: the Cagliari lagoon, the Molentargius-Saline park, which you can visit on a mountain bike, to see the pink flamingos take flight, and, of course, the sea.

Take a dip at Poetto, the city's 8 km long soft sandy beach along which there is a walking trail and cycling path. Even at night, when it reveals its more glamorous side, it is a delight. You can take an excursion to Calamosca and Sella del Diavolo from Poetto. And, finally, there is the local cuisine to be enjoyed, spaghetti with bottarga (cured mullet or tuna roe) and artichokes, burrida made with catshark and walnuts, and fregula con cocciula, balls of semola with clams.

Nuoro

Nuoro is the Athens of Sardinia, bustling with cultural life since the 1800s, home to artists like Salvatore and Sebastiano Satta, Francesco Ciusa and the author Grazia Deledda, who made the city famous the world over. A stroll through the historical centre is a relaxing pastime, a step back in time as you walk over ages-old cobblestones along streets lined with old stone houses, courtyards, porticos and little squares that seem to appear out of nowhere.

Among the old quarters is Séuna, once home to farmers and craftsmen, and santu Pedru, where shepherds and landowners lived. It is here that you will find the Deledda Museum, the birthplace of the Nobel prize winner. The house is an homage to the memory of this author who opened Sardinia up to the world. She lies at rest in the little church della Solitudine at the feet of the Ortobene, city's mountain or, as she defined it, "our soul," a natural park well worth a visit.

Corso Garibaldi used to be called Via Majore and has always been the social hub of the city, with shops and timeless cafés. Have a coffee at one of the outdoor tables there, then stroll about the narrow streets and enjoy a meal in one of the many characteristic restaurants or trattorias. Not far away is the old delle Grazie church, and the majestic Cathedral of Santa Maria della Neve. Next to it is a belvedere that leads to the Tribu cultural centre and the Ciusa Museum, home to many fascinating sculptures made by Francesco Ciusa, the first prize winner of the 1907 Venice Bienniale.

The Museo d'Arte di Nuoro (MAN) is a short walk away and hosts temporary international exhibitions and permanent shows of XX century Sardinian artists. Also not to be missed is the Museum of Sardinian Life and Popular Traditions, which will give you a taste of material and immaterial culture through displays of garments, jewellery, masks, textiles, tools and references to traditional singing, religious practices and festivities. Don't miss seeing costumes like these in actual use during the sagra del Redentore on the last Sunday of August, featuring folk groups from all over Sardinia.

The celebrations include a procession of the faithful walking from the city to Ortobene, at the top of which, at altitude of about 1,000m, is the statue of Christ the

Redeemer (the Redentore). The 1,600 hectares of the mountain boasts traces of settlements dating back to prehistoric times, like the domus de Janas, as well as an infinity of gorgeous scenery, like Sedda Ortai park. Granite rock formations of unusual shapes hover interspersed between valleys, the home of a variety of mammals and rare birds of prey.

Tortolì

Tortolì is the port of Ogliastra, the gateway to a surprising world with a wide variety of landscapes. Around the city, where 11,000 people live and to which tens of thousands of tourists flock in summer, you'll find tropical beaches, dense woods and Mediterranean brush, fertile plains and marshes, gently rolling hills covered in tilled fields and an oddity, a wide stripe of porphyry red rock that runs parallel to the coastline.

The Rocce Rosse, literally red rocks, in the Arbatax area are the most spectacular example of this phenomenon, a natural monument that sticks straight up out of the emerald blue sea along the shore offering a truly amazing colour contrast. It is here that the Rocce Rosse Blues festival is held. The adjacent harbour is where the tourists arrive and take off on excursions to explore the enchanting coves and inlets of Ogliastra.

The sea around Tortolì is magnificent, it is the shoreline that has most often been awarded the FEE's Blue Flag. Behind the Rocce Rosse is Cala Moresca, the city's pride and joy, a beach of golden sand edged with granite boulders. A bit further south you'll find the many shades of blue of Porto Frailis and the long Lido di Orrì beach: sixteen kilometres of hidden coves and little beaches, including the lovely Cala Ginepro, blessed with fine sand, polished pebbles and a stand of juniper trees, and San Gemiliano. The red rocks also appear in the little slice of heaven that is Cea, four kilometres of soft white beaches. This spectacle of nature is complemented by lovely green areas: like the town's La Sughereta park and Batteria park, perched on the top of a hill with views over the entire gulf.

There are more than 200 monuments here that date back to the Nuragic Age, and the s'Ortali 'e su Monti is an exemplary site. Its seven hectares includes a Nuragic complex, a Giant's Tomb, two menhirs, huts, a domu de Janas chamber tomb, a wall and the remains of another nuraghe. The port of Sulci Tirrenica was built to accommodate navigators with the arrival of the Phoenicians (VII century BCE) and the Punic peoples.

Traces of Punic settlement were found in the marshes of Tortolì, while vestiges of Roman domination take the form of shipwrecks in the depths of the gulf. The ancient control towers, like the torre di San Miguel, were built by the Spaniards. The city's landmarks include the su Logu de s'Iscultura museum of modern art and the former Cathedral of Sant'Andrea, a classic building from the XVIII century built over an older church. Two chapels of the older church remain, and in one of them they found the simulacrum of St. Elisabeth of Hungary. Inside the church is an elaborate altar of multi-coloured marble. The town's most heartfelt festival is Stella Maris in late July at the church of Arbatax and features a procession that leads to the water's edge.

While in the area, make sure to eat some culurgiones, typical ravioli, the stews, porcetto, roast lamb and boiled sheep meat along with a glass of cannonau, the most authentic of Ogliastra's experiences.

Villasimius

The intense colours of the sea, the glimmering crystal-clear water, granite cliffs, enchanting coves, long stretches of beach, lagoons and verdant hills, some of them are the settings of TV ads and all of them are breathtaking. Villasimius is the 'pearl' of the south, the kind of tourist resort every vacationer dreams of, with a population of less than 4,000 during winter that blossoms to several tens of thousands in summer. The coastline is graced with a crown of beaches interspersed with inlets and the Capo Carbonara promontory.

Along the panoramic road starting at Capo Boi, the southernmost point of the protected Marine Area, are the wonderful beaches of Porto sa Ruxi, Campus and Campulongu, all blessed with gorgeous blue seas and white sandy beaches framed by Mediterranean brush. Not far from town is the unusual spiaggia del Riso beach, remarkable for its rice-shaped sand. Past the modern-day tourist harbour, on the western side of

Capo Carbonara, are inlets nestled between the cliffs, including Cala Caterina.

On the eastern side are other breathtaking gems of the seashore, starting with Porto Giunco, and behind it the stagno di Notteri marshes where pink flamingos and other rare species of wild birds nest. From high up on the promontory that looks out over it, home to an Aragonese tower built by Spaniards, is an amazing panorama with will linger in your mind, your heart and your pictures for ever: an endless field of shades of blue, two seas divided by a narrow strip of white sand that looks like powdered sugar.

Further north are the beaches of Simius and Traias, followed by Rio Trottu and Manunzas, that provide the backdrop for Punta Molentis, another 'gem' of Villasimius. From Capo Boi to the Island of Serpentara, the isola dei Cavoli and shoals that are the resting places of shipwrecks from all eras, the Capo Carbonara marine reserve is rich in underwater treasures: dense schools of fish move like weightless clouds over meadows of gently waving sea grass, over bastions, into valleys and channels coloured yellow by sea daisies and red by sea fans.

Back on land you can go shopping, enjoy delicious seafood, visit museums and pick over archaeological sites. Go see remains dating to the Nuragic age, tour the Accu Is Traias (I century BCE III century CE) and Cruccuris (I-II CE) necropoles near the roman baths of Santa Maria, and the Cuccureddus site, an early Phoenician-Punic settlement later taken over by the Romans. And don't miss the archaeological museum, with displays about the treasures that lie at the bottom of the sea. One of these, the statue of the Virgin of the Sea, lies on the bottom near Cavoli island. It was sculpted by Pinuccio Sciola and every year in late July they have the Festa della Madonna del Naufrago to commemorate those who lost their lives at sea with a procession that leads to the water's edge.

Chia

The ancient village of Chia, an important Phoenician and then Roman centre named Bithia, was in a small cove where today there is one of the many coastal towers built in the seventeenth century by the Spanish crown against the incursions of the Barbary pirates. Among the ruins brought to light following a storm, there are the remains of a *Punic Tophet* and the ancient road that connected it to the important city of Nora. Today it is the destination for trekking and mountain bike enthusiasts who can travel the dirt road that runs along the old road, enjoying particularly fascinating coastal stretches.

From the tower, overlooking the coast, there is access to a long stretch of sand interspersed with small coves framed by dense vegetation and lapped by an emerald-green sea, a true spectacle of nature that remains forever in the hearts of any visitor.

Along the coast to the west you pass the beaches of Sa Tuerra, Porto Campana Spiaggia de su Sali, and Su Giudeu the most beautiful of all. Also known as the *spiaggia de s'Abba Durci* (fresh water beach), it is a long stretch of white sand surrounded by high dunes covered with juniper trees, which, with their shapes create a particularly evocative landscape.

On the back of this stretch of coastline lies the Spartivento pond, precious natural oasis habitat for many animal species. In front of the beach of Giudeu, a short distance from the shore, there is an island within easy reach due to shallow waters that separate it from the mainland. Thanks to its special charm, this beach is often chosen as a natural backdrop for films and TV commercials.

On the westernmost part of this coast is the Cala Cipolla beach. Only accessible on foot, it extends around a small cove sheltered and enclosed by a rocky promontory that separates it from the more extensive coastline. From Cala Cipolla there is a scenic path that lets you reach the Faro di Capo Spartivento, whose summit dominates the whole southern coast of Sulcis.

With their shallow waters, all the beaches along the Chia coast are particularly frequented by families with children and by underwater fishing and diving enthusiasts. Often beaten by the mistral wind, Chia is also an ideal destination for surfers who can perform spectacular stunts. Rich in tourist services, these beaches are accessible to the disabled and have ample parking.

Castelsardo

It may have been the legendary Tibula of Roman times, but by the Middle Ages it was already an impenetrable centuries-old fortress protected by thick walls and 17 towers, until the advent of modern weaponry. The original nucleus of Castelsardo grew up around the castle of the Dorias, which tradition dates to 1102, although it was probably constructed in the late XIII century. Today it is the seat of the lovely Museo dell'Intreccio Mediterraneo (or Museum of the Crossroads of the Mediterranean), one of the most visited museums in all of Sardinia. In the early XVI century the castle was renamed Castillo Aragonés and became the seat of the bishopric until the Cathedral of Sant'Antonio Abate was built in 1586.

This amazing building has a bell tower perched over the sea, is graced with a gleaming ceramic dome and houses crypts in the basement, which in turn are home to the Maestro di Castelsardo museum. During the reign of the Savoy dynasty, the town was given the name it has today. It belongs to the Most Beautiful Towns of Italy Association and its noble fortifications the bastions and steep stairs remain intact. The city tour includes not-to-be-missed visits of its religious and historical buildings, like the Church of Santa Maria delle Grazie, the Benedictine monastery, the bishopric, palazzo La Loggia, which since 1111 has served as City Hall, and the Palazzo Eleonora d'Arborea.

The town's most characteristic events take place during Holy Week, when religious rites with a Spanish flair involve just about everyone. Lunissanti, on the Monday after Palm Sunday, is heartfelt and picturesque, especially at dawn when a long procession heads towards the Basilica of Nostra Signora di Tergu. After sundown, the town is illuminated by torches and sacred chanting fills the air.

The Prucissioni that take place on Holy Thursday and the Lu Lcravamentu on Friday are also not to be missed. The town celebrates its patron saint, St. Anthony, on 17 January with great bonfires. But there is more to this town than cultural tradition, there are archaeological sites and natural monuments to be visited as well: the nuraghe Paddaju, the pre-Nuragic megalithic walls at Monte Ossoni and, just four kilometres from town, the domus de Janas, raised bull horn decorations and the roccia dell'Elefante.

This stretch of shoreline is made predominantly of high red bluffs, but there are some beaches too, including Marina di Castelsardo, at the entrance to town, and Lu Bagnu beach, some two and a half kilometres away and protected by cliffs topped with green. The sandy shore boasts crystal clear water dotted with flat rocks. Windsurf and sailing enthusiasts should not miss punta La Capra, a natural pool set between the sea and the shore. Local restaurants feature fresh catch: lobster, crayfish, crab, sea urchin and shellfish.

Stintino

The true wonder of Stintino is the coast: a necklace of white beaches and a nature oasis. Make sure and see La Pelosa Beach: shallow waters, impalpable sand, a Spanish tower and the dazzling, calm blue sea. Visit Cape Falcone, a promontory of rugged beauty, where peregrine falcons look after their fledglings in wild ravines. Two hundred meters up, a terrace offers a spectacular view of Asinara Island, Isola Piana and the coast.

The place is unique for its double view of the seascape: to the west, on the Outside Sea, it's dark and wild and swept by the wind; to the east, on the Inside Sea, clear blue waters fringe the pure white edges of the coast. The town was built in 1885 on a small fjord, when the

Italian government set up a leper hospital and penal colony there; hence the name s'isthintinu, meaning gut. And so it was that the "Communion of 45", a cooperative of fishermen and their families, gave birth to a flourishing town.

Near the village are the ancient tuna traps, which until the twentieth century were the main source of income for the town; they are now restored and will greet you with their historic charm united with the blue sea. At about 3 km from the town center, hidden between the hills and the sea, is the pond of Casaraccio, home to numerous species of birds such as cormorants, larks, terns and egrets. Stintino's culinary tradition is based almost exclusively on fish: urchins, shellfish, mussels and clams are the treasure of its narrow streets and alleys, along with tuna roe and Stintino style octopus. If you love to practice or watch Latin Sail regattas, this is your paradise for sure!

Bosa

Bosa is a fabulous village where history and modernity come together generating curiosity and fascination.

The Old Village, also known as Sa Costa, lies around the Serravalle Castle, built by the Malaspinas between the twelfth and thirteenth centuries. Easily accessible on foot, it will reward you by showing you the charm of the town from a scenic location that will remain forever in your memory.

Bosa Marina is instead the beach resort most loved by tourists according to Blue Guide 2015, which gives it a record 5 sails including it among the places with the most beautiful sea. The poetic Lungotemo promenade with the Ponte Vecchio and the beaches of S'Abba Druche, Portu Managu, Turas and Cumpoltitu make it one of the most renowned places for natural beauty.

Bosa is also a place of great culinary and craftsmanship tradition that welcomes you with a fine glass of Malvasia. The excellences of the village include jewelry from coral fished in the sea, baskets of Asphodel, fabrics and the filet of ancient feminine knowledge.

You will find many churches and monuments in the Village. Spend a little time at the Church of the Immaculate Conception, the town's Cathedral, featuring beautiful frescoes. Within the walls of Serravalle castle stands the church of Our Lady de Sos Regnos Altos, embellished with a set of frescoes dating back to 1370. The Romanesque church of San Pietro Extramuros stands a short distance from the village, in the rural locality of Calmedia. Make sure to take a stroll in the medieval district of Sa Costa and take pictures of Sa funtana manna, a nineteenth century monument made of red trachyte.

If you enjoy hiking or birdwatching, you will love the natural wealth offered by Capo Marrargiu Bio-marine Park and the Nature Reserve of Badde Aggiosu, Marrargiu and Monte Mannu.

Bosa is also famous for its Carnival, known as Karrasegare. The "S'Attitidu" procession features a group of black masks lamenting theatrically while holding a doll in their arms, symbolizing the newly born holiday.

Alghero

With its 44,000 inhabitants, it is the 5th largest city of Sardinia. Alghero is the island's main harbour town, home to Fertilia airport and one of its best-loved cities for the popular walkway along the port's bastions, the red roofs that touch the sky and the gorgeous natural bay that flows into the emerald sea. The shoreline is some 90 km long and known as the Coral Riviera, home to a major colony of the finest coral.

The most famous beach here is Le Bombarde, blessed with crystalline water and a clean sandy bottom, it is a favourite destination of families, young people and surfing enthusiasts. Just a kilometre away is Lazzaretto, ten inlets with soft sandy beaches. A bit further away in the bay of Porto Conte is the leisurely Mugoni beach, graced with golden sand and the still waters of a sea that is always calm and crystalline, a completely protected oasis.

The shoreline at the city's centre, on the other hand, is home to the splendid Lido di San Giovanni beach, while just outside of town are the Maria Pia dunes, dotted with centuries-old juniper trees. Much of the coastline is within the protected marine zone of Capo Caccia – Isola Piana, where hundreds of treasures are safeguarded, including the grotta di Nettuno, which can be reached over land via the Escala del Cabriol, and by sea with boats that depart from the harbour.

The Porto Conte park will amaze you with its expanses of Mediterranean brush, dense woods and the laguna del Calich. The domus de Janas of santu Perdu, the Anghelu Ruju necropolis and the complexes of Palmavera and sant'Imbenia bear witness to Alghero's prehistoric origins, starting in the Neolithic era.

The historical centre is the city's most interesting area, a labyrinth of narrow streets that connect piazzas bustling with life. The yellow walls and ancient houses echo the Catalan origins of the city. As do the churches: the Cathedral of Santa Maria (XVI century), the churches of Carmelo (late XVII century) with its great gilded retablo, that of San Michele with its coloured ceramic dome, and the late Renaissance Sant'Anna (1735).

If it's culture you're after, then visit Casa Manno, a research centre full of important paintings, furniture, books and manuscripts. Alghero is famous for its fine coral, which is used locally with gold to make every manner of adornment. Do stop in at the Museo del Corallo and learn more about the history of coral and how it is used. The big event in 2017 will be the opening race of the great multi-city Giro d'Italia cycling event. Another great time to be here is at Cap d'Any de l'Alguer, or "New Years at Alghero," when a myriad of shows enliven the city centre. The most passionate time of year is Holy Week, with heartfelt religious rites from the Spanish tradition.

Weather

The mild climate of Sardinia
Sardinia has a maritime Mediterranean climate, stronger along the coastal strip, due to its insularity

and to the small distance from sea of every part of its territory. It is temperate during all the year.

It naturally shows the effects of its geographical position (in the centre of Mediterranean sea). In fact, the Island is situated in the trajectory of tropical air masses coming from the African coasts on one side, and air masses carried by Western winds originate from the Atlantic Ocean on the other side. It is sporadically crossed by cold currents of air coming from the Artic.

Normally the North is more rainy than the South. In winter, the temperature is normally around 10° C in the coastal cities and a little bit lower in the inland area, while during the summer it can reach and exceed 30° C.

The summer tends to be more or less long depending on the year, but it is usually possible to spend a nice day at the beach (bath included) from April to October.

Winds

A climate element of valuable significance is constituted by winds. Actually the island is crossed, during all the year, by winds coming from all directions.

The dominant wind during the winter season is the Mistral, a North-West wind. Along the coastal strips, protected by no mountains, the Maestrale has left indelible signs in the landscape. It eroded and modelled the rocks, and deformed the trees which assumed an inclined position towards South-East.

Another winter wind is Libeccio (it blows from South-West), which invests all the Western strip, going North beyond the Bocche di Bonifacio and South, along the Sulcis, till it reaches the Cagliari Gulf.

Moreover, the Sirocco, a hot and originally dry wind, originates from African deserts, that while crossing the sea overloads on humidity, and when it invests Sardinia it carries humid air.

Levant is less frequent, it usually reaches the Eastern coast still fresh and enough humid.

Minor winds are the North wind and Grecale (East wind), either cool in summer or in winter. Rains, which have a sporadic and stormy character, are not a very frequent event, especially in the coastal zones.

Discover the island: Typical Products

Typical products
Sardinian cuisine is simple and comes from the farming and dairy activities. Indeed, it is based on four elements, namely bread, cheese, milk and meat.

Traditional bread
The most popular bread is the one named "carasau", thin round biscuit-like layers (yeast-free) that can be kept for long periods. As a result, it is eaten by shepherds during the transhumance, thus being the

typical inland food. There are also different types of soft bread, differing in taste and smell: beside spianata Ozierese, very similar to Carasau bread, there are different kinds of crumb bread such as the Campidanese round loaf, the civraxiu and the coccoi.

Sardinian cheese

Sardinians have been the masters of dairy products since Carthaginians, Phoenicians, Romans as evidenced by worldwide appreciation of Sardinian cheese and award of popular DOP brand (high-quality product). Pecorino is the king of sardinian cheeses. To be defined as such, it has to be produced with sheep milk only. It can be enjoyed alone, or for seasoning. It is excellent for seasoning "malloreddus", (semolina gnocchi - a kind of pasta - seasoned with pork fat sausage). Fresh pecorino and ricotta, another fine dairy product, are also used to make delicious pastries.

Meat and Fish

Meat, usually pork, is often roasted in the "a carraxu" way, an old way of cooking the whole animal wrapped in sweet herbs over a fire for four or five hours. Fish is also excellent in Sardinia: the recipes are delicious and exquisite. We advise freshly-caught fish and the typical Oristano botargo and merca.

WINES
Typical dishes must be accompanied by typical island wine, the best being Cannonau and Vermentino. Sardinia has always boasted diffused vineyards even though cultivated in special regions. From different places were imported vines that, over the centuries, originated typical wines such as Oristano's Vernaccia or Sardinia's Cannonau. Vine growing developed primarily along the coast and plains; inside, along with Campidano, there are just few towns or hamlets with vine growing surface areas exceeding 500 hectares including Oliena and Ierzu, two geographic sub-

denominations, along with Capo Ferrato, of Sardinia's Cannonau.

Cagliari's Nuragus, Gallura's and Sardinia's Vermentino fulfill the growing demand for fresh light wine.

ermentino is unique due to particular production rules: vineyards should be under 500 meters in height, with at least 3,300 plants per hectare and yields not exceeding three kilograms per vine. It is straw-yellow with greenish streaks, with thin penetrating smell reminiscent of the Mediterranean Scrub. Dry, with a sourish aftertaste, it is perfect for fish and tuna, cheese, botargo, the main Sardinian speciality.

Sweets and pastries
Among the traditional sardinian sweets, the mostt common are the seadas (fresh-pasta fritters stuffed with cheese and topped with sour honey, tiricche (grape or fig-based), papassini (glace rhombus-shaped

biscuits), formaggelle (round pastry of fresh pecorino or ricotta, seasoned with sugar,

www.ingramcontent.com/pod-product-compliance
Lightning Source LLC
Chambersburg PA
CBHW021105080526
44587CB00010B/382